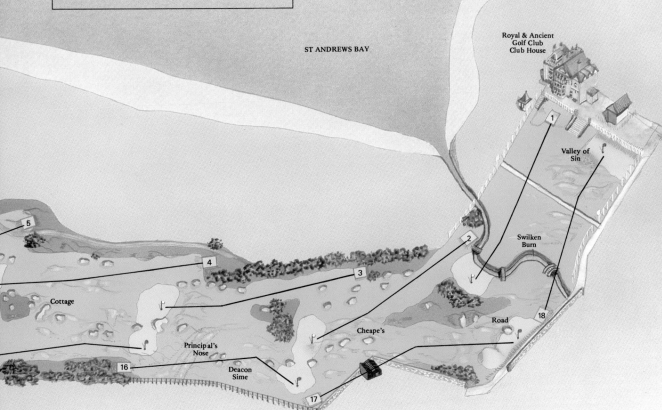

124TH OPEN CHAMPIONSHIP
Card of the Old Course

Hole	Par	Yards	Hole	Par	Yards
1	4	370	10	4	342
2	4	411	11	3	172
3	4	371	12	4	316
4	4	463	13	4	425
5	5	564	14	5	567
6	4	416	15	4	413
7	4	372	16	4	382
8	3	178	17	4	461
9	4	356	18	4	354
Out	36	3,501	In	36	3,432
			Total	72	6,933

ST ANDREWS BAY

Royal & Ancient
Golf Club
Club House

Valley of
Sin

Swilken
Burn

Road

Cottage

Principal's
Nose

Cheape's

Deacon
Sime

THE OPEN CHAMPIONSHIP
1995

OFFICIAL ANNUAL
PRESENTED IN ASSOCIATION WITH

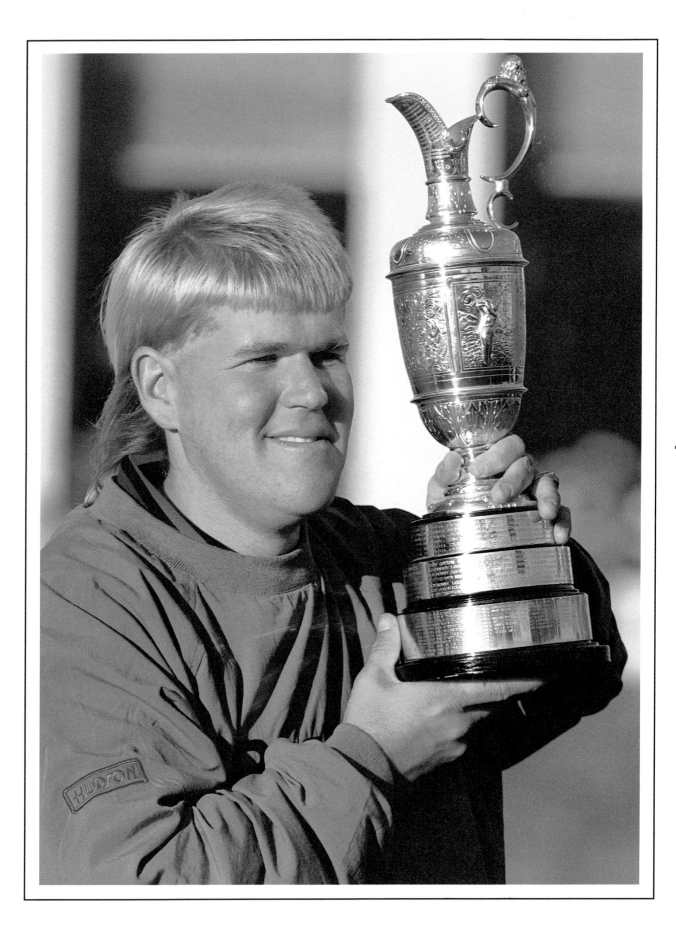

THE OPEN CHAMPIONSHIP 1995

WRITERS

ROBERT SOMMERS
MICHAEL MCDONNELL
RAYMOND JACOBS
MICHAEL WILLIAMS
ALISTER NICOL
JOHN HOPKINS

PHOTOGRAPHERS

MICHAEL COHEN
FRED VUICH

EDITOR

BEV NORWOOD

AUTHORISED BY THE
CHAMPIONSHIP COMMITTEE
OF THE ROYAL AND ANCIENT
GOLF CLUB OF ST ANDREWS

THE CONTRIBUTORS DEDICATE THIS BOOK TO
THE MEMORY OF LAWRENCE LEVY (1947-1995).

TRANSWORLD PUBLISHERS LTD
61-63 Uxbridge Road, London W5 5SA

TRANSWORLD PUBLISHERS (AUSTRALIA) PTY LTD
15-23 Helles Avenue, Moorebank, NSW 2170

TRANSWORLD PUBLISHERS (NZ) LTD
Cnr Moselle and Waipareira Aves,
Henderson, Auckland

Published 1995 by Partridge Press
a division of Transworld Publishers Ltd
Copyright © 1995 The Championship Committee Merchandising
Limited

Statistics of 124th Open Championship produced on a
Unisys Computer System

Fred Vuich is staff photographer for GOLF Magazine (USA)
and photographs are courtesy of Times Mirror Magazines, Inc.
Photographs on pp. 14-22 courtesy of Brian Morgan
Photograph on p. 83 (top) courtesy of Kirstie Morgan
Photographs on pp. 23-25 courtesy of Allsport Photographic plc

A CIP catalogue record for this book is available
from the British Library

185225 2243

Typeset by Davis Design
Printed in Great Britain
by Bath Press Colourbooks, Glasgow

CONTENTS

INTRODUCTION

BY R. H. EVANS, C. B. E.
Chief Executive
British Aerospace plc

The Open Championship returned to St Andrews and the home of golf for the first time since 1990 when Nick Faldo triumphed so splendidly for his second Championship victory.

The Old Course and the historic 'auld toon' again provided the most wonderful setting for international golfers and spectators alike, and British Aerospace were delighted to welcome so many customers and friends from around the world to this historic venue.

For British Aerospace, a world force in the aerospace industry, the Open Championship provides the perfect setting to grow customer relationships and thus future business.

John Daly, the eventual winner, and Costantino Rocca provided us all with great drama over the closing holes and in the subsequent play-off. British Aerospace will look forward to another great Championship in 1996 at Royal Lytham, a Lancashire venue said by many top players to be the toughest of all challenges.

R. H. Evans, C. B. E.

THE CHAMPIONSHIP COMMITTEE

CHAIRMAN

P. W. J. GREENHOUGH

DEPUTY CHAIRMAN

D. J. HARRISON

COMMITTEE

A. BRODIE
J. E. COOK
R. M. E. DAVITT
M. C. GRINT
A. J. HILL
G. B. HOBART
G. HUDDY
R. H. PALMER
R. P. WHITE
R. S. WHITMORE

BUSINESS SUB-COMMITTEE CHAIRMAN

A. W. DICKIE

RULES SUB-COMMITTEE CHAIRMAN

W. J. F. BRYCE

ADDITIONAL MEMBER

G. B. OVENS
COUNCIL OF NATIONAL GOLF UNIONS

SECRETARY

M. F. BONALLACK, OBE

DEPUTY SECRETARY

W. G. WILSON

CHAMPIONSHIP SECRETARY

D. HILL

ASSISTANT SECRETARY (CHAMPIONSHIPS)

D. R. WEIR

CHAMPIONSHIP ASSISTANT

A. E. FARQUHAR

INTRODUCTION

BY P. W. J. GREENHOUGH
Chairman of Championship Committee
Royal and Ancient Golf Club of St Andrews

The 124th Open Championship will be remembered for the wind, a near Italian triumph, Arnold Palmer's farewell and a play-off.

Walter Woods, the Links Superintendent, retires at the end of this year but made certain that the course was in superb condition. The course was greener than normal but there was plenty of run and the combination of wind and sun soon ensured the fairways and greens presented the players with a suitable challenge.

Over 1,800 players entered the Championship, but finally it came down to a play-off between John Daly and Costantino Rocca. The need for a play-off arose from a remarkable putt by Rocca after a less-than-memorable second at the 72nd hole. John Daly produced a display of power golf allied to a magical short game — a worthy champion.

The Championship Committee are grateful to the St Andrews Links Management Trust and the local Clubs for the help and assistance they gave throughout the Championship.

We also wish to acknowledge the continued support of British Aerospace in the publication of this official record, and we thank the photographers and writers who have helped to record a memorable Championship within its pages.

P. W. J. Greenhough

Peter Greenhough.

FOREWORD

BY JOHN DALY

I came to St Andrews with a good feeling because I had played well in the Alfred Dunhill Cup two years ago. Before I came over that time, Lee Trevino told me if I would ever win the Open, it would be on the Old Course. While it was only my fourth appearance in the Open Championship I had very positive feelings toward the Old Course.

Everyone assumed I would like the Old Course because of its wide fairways, but what truly impressed me on that first trip were those long putts and shots around the green you needed to make. To win at St Andrews would require a complete golf game, and of course, some good fortune.

It was incredible to win the Open Championship and to win at St Andrews is a lifetime dream for all golfers. It is an awesome feeling to see my name on the trophy with the great names of the past. I thought I was perhaps too impatient and too inexperienced to win on links courses, but in the end I was crowned champion of the 1995 Open Championship at St Andrews. I am very proud of this accomplishment and look forward to defending my championship at Royal Lytham in 1996.

John Daly

124TH OPEN CHAMPIONSHIP

*Denotes amateurs

NAME	SCORES				TOTAL	MONEY
John Daly, USA	67	71	73	71	282	£125,000
Costantino Rocca, Italy	69	70	70	73	282	100,000
Steven Bottomley, England	70	72	72	69	283	65,667
Mark Brooks, USA	70	69	73	71	283	65,667
Michael Campbell, New Zealand	71	71	65	76	283	65,667
Vijay Singh, Fiji	68	72	73	71	284	40,500
Steve Elkington, Australia	72	69	69	74	284	40,500
Mark James, England	72	75	68	70	285	33,333
Bob Estes, USA	72	70	71	72	285	33,333
Corey Pavin, USA	69	70	72	74	285	33,333
Payne Stewart, USA	72	68	75	71	286	26,000
Brett Ogle, Australia	73	69	71	73	286	26,000
Sam Torrance, Scotland	71	70	71	74	286	26,000
Ernie Els, South Africa	71	68	72	75	286	26,000
Greg Norman, Australia	71	74	72	70	287	18,200
Robert Allenby, Australia	71	74	71	71	287	18,200
Ben Crenshaw, USA	67	72	76	72	287	18,200
Per-Ulrik Johansson, Sweden	69	78	68	72	287	18,200
Brad Faxon, USA	71	67	75	74	287	18,200
Peter Mitchell, England	73	74	71	70	288	13,500
David Duval, USA	71	75	70	72	288	13,500
Andrew Coltart, Scotland	70	74	71	73	288	13,500
Barry Lane, England	72	73	68	75	288	13,500
Lee Janzen, USA	73	73	71	72	289	10,317
* Steven Webster, England	70	72	74	73	289	Medal
Bernhard Langer, Germany	72	71	73	73	289	10,317
Jesper Parnevik, Sweden	75	71	70	73	289	10,317
Mark Calcavecchia, USA	71	72	72	74	289	10,317
Bill Glasson, USA	68	74	72	75	289	10,317
Katsuyoshi Tomori, Japan	70	68	73	78	289	10,317
Ross Drummond, Scotland	74	68	77	71	290	8,122
Jose Maria Olazabal, Spain	72	72	74	72	290	8,122
David Frost, South Africa	72	72	74	72	290	8,122
Hisayuki Sasaki, Japan	74	71	72	73	290	8,122
John Huston, USA	71	74	72	73	290	8,122
Peter Jacobsen, USA	71	76	70	73	290	8,122
Darren Clarke, N. Ireland	69	77	70	74	290	8,122
David Feherty, N. Ireland	68	75	71	76	290	8,122
Tom Watson, USA	67	76	70	77	290	8,122
Severiano Ballesteros, Spain	75	69	76	71	291	7,050
Warren Bennett, England	72	74	73	72	291	7,050
Phil Mickelson, USA	70	71	77	73	291	7,050
Mark McNulty, Zimbabwe	67	76	74	74	291	7,050
Nick Faldo, England	74	67	75	75	291	7,050
Brian Watts, USA	72	71	73	75	291	7,050
* Gordon Sherry, Scotland	70	71	74	76	291	
John Cook, USA	69	70	75	77	291	7,050
Nick Price, Zimbabwe	70	74	70	77	291	7,050
Ian Woosnam, Wales	71	74	76	71	292	6,350
Anders Forsbrand, Sweden	70	74	75	73	292	6,350
Mark O'Meara, USA	72	72	75	73	292	6,350
Tsuneyuki Nakajima, Japan	73	72	72	75	292	6,350
Brian Claar, USA	71	75	71	75	292	6,350
Ken Green, USA	71	72	73	76	292	6,350
Jim Gallagher Jnr, USA	69	76	75	73	293	5,900
Peter O'Malley, Australia	71	73	74	75	293	5,900
Russell Claydon, England	70	74	71	78	293	5,900

NAME		SCORES			TOTAL	MONEY
Peter Senior, Australia	71	75	78	70	294	5,475
Paul Broadhurst, England	73	72	76	73	294	5,475
Derrick Cooper, England	71	76	74	73	294	5,475
Eduardo Herrera, Colombia	74	72	73	75	294	5,475
Tom Kite, USA	72	76	71	75	294	5,475
Paul Lawrie, Scotland	73	71	74	76	294	5,475
Martin Gates, England	73	73	72	76	294	5,475
Raymond Floyd, USA	72	74	72	76	294	5,475
Justin Leonard, USA	73	67	77	77	294	5,475
David Gilford, England	69	72	75	78	294	5,475
Peter Baker, England	70	74	81	70	295	4,975
Jeff Maggert, USA	75	70	78	72	295	4,975
Jonathan Lomas, England	74	73	75	73	295	4,975
Frank Nobilo, New Zealand	70	71	80	74	295	4,975
Gary Player, South Africa	71	73	77	74	295	4,975
Olle Karlsson, Sweden	71	76	73	75	295	4,975
Mats Hallberg, Sweden	68	76	75	76	295	4,975
Scott Hoch, USA	74	72	73	76	295	4,975
Gary Hallberg, USA	72	74	72	77	295	4,975
Jose Rivero, Spain	70	72	75	78	295	4,975
* Tiger Woods, USA	74	71	72	78	295	
Ryoken Kawagishi, Japan	72	76	80	68	296	4,500
Patrick Burke, USA	75	72	78	71	296	4,500
Jack Nicklaus, USA	78	70	77	71	296	4,500
Bob Lohr, USA	76	68	79	73	296	4,500
Jarmo Sandelin, Sweden	75	71	77	73	296	4,500
Sandy Lyle, Scotland	71	71	79	75	296	4,500
Steve Lowery, USA	69	74	76	77	296	4,500
Dean Robertson, Scotland	71	73	74	78	296	4,500
Jay Haas, USA	76	72	70	78	296	4,500
Miguel Angel Jimenez, Spain	75	73	76	73	297	4,125
Mark Davis, England	74	71	76	76	297	4,125
Jay Delsing, USA	72	75	73	77	297	4,125
Eduardo Romero, Argentina	74	74	72	77	297	4,125
Gene Sauers, USA	69	73	75	80	297	4,125
Wayne Riley, Australia	70	72	75	80	297	4,125
John Hawksworth, England	73	74	75	76	298	4,000
Bill Longmuir, Scotland	72	76	72	78	298	4,000
Lee Westwood, England	71	72	82	74	299	4,000
Jose Coceres, Argentina	71	76	78	74	299	4,000
Simon Burnell, England	72	76	75	77	300	4,000
Davis Love III, USA	70	78	74	78	300	4,000
* Gary Clark, England	71	76	80	74	301	
Don Pooley, USA	76	71	80	75	302	4,000
Mark Nichols, England	75	68	78	81	302	4,000
Pedro Linhart, Spain	72	75	77	79	303	4,000

NON QUALIFIERS AFTER 36 HOLES
(All professionals receive £650)

John Watson, England	76 73	149
Bob Tway, USA	71 78	149
Paul Azinger, USA	74 75	149
Mike Springer, USA	75 74	149
Masashi Ozaki, Japan	70 79	149
Bob Charles, New Zealand	73 76	149
Scott Simpson, USA	72 77	149
Howard Clark, England	76 73	149
John Morse, USA	75 74	149
Curtis Strange, USA	73 76	149
Peter Fowler, Australia	74 75	149
Nigel Graves, England	72 77	149
Jamie Spence, England	77 73	150
Mark Roe, England	75 75	150
Stephen Leaney, Australia	76 74	150
Loren Roberts, USA	76 74	150
Wayne Grady, Australia	75 75	150
Tony Johnstone, Zimbabwe	75 75	150

Brandt Jobe, USA	74 76	150
Colin Montgomerie, Scotland	75 75	150
Craig Stadler, USA	74 76	150
Mark McCumber, USA	73 77	150
Miguel Martin, Spain	73 77	150
Michel Besanceney, France	73 77	150
Larry Mize, USA	74 77	151
Tom Weiskopf, USA	76 75	151
Michael Clayton, Australia	74 77	151
Andrew Crerar, Scotland	77 74	151
* Stephen Gallacher, Scotland	72 79	151
Tom Wargo, USA	72 79	151
Robert Karlsson, Sweden	77 74	151
Paul Carman, England	72 79	151
John Bickerton, England	71 80	151
Brad Bryant, USA	78 74	152
Carl Mason, England	75 77	152
Billy Andrade, USA	76 76	152
Lee Trevino, USA	75 77	152
Ian Baker-Finch, Australia	77 76	153

Tohru Suzuki, Japan	80 73	153
Ronan Rafferty, N. Ireland	75 78	153
Adam Tillman, England	75 78	153
John Wither, Scotland	75 78	153
Mathias Gronberg, Sweden	81 72	153
Kazuhiro Takami, Japan	76 77	153
Craig Parry, Australia	76 77	153
Russell Weir, Scotland	71 82	153
Neil Roderick, Wales	74 79	153
Richard Boxall, England	72 81	153
Fredrik Andersson, Sweden	77 76	153
Martyn Thompson, England	76 79	155
Arnold Palmer, USA	83 75	158
Brandel Chamblee, USA	80 78	158
Paul Mayo, Wales	77 82	159
Gary Stafford, England	78 84	162
Andrew Oldcorn, England	73	Retd
Philip Walton, Ireland	75	Retd

The links stretch from the town along St Andrews Bay and round the Eden estuary.

ROUND THE OLD COURSE

No. 1 370 Yards, Par 4

The fairway is 200 yards wide but still demands an accurate tee shot so that the approach across the Swilcan Burn, which guards the front of the green, has the best angle of attack at a flagstick invariably tucked close to the water's edge.

No. 2 411 Yards, Par 4

The massive undulations on this green dictate the best approach so that tee shots should favour the right side of the fairway. But the general St Andrews rule applies: err on the side of length with the approach because most of the trouble is in front of the green.

No. 3 371 Yards, Par 4

The ideal line is to the right but beware of the pot bunkers and bushes. With the pin invariably protected by Cartgate Bunker, the smart approach is away from the pin so as to allow the contours of the green itself to bring the ball closer to the target.

No. 4 463 Yards, Par 4

There is a choice of tee shots either to the right between bunkers or a bank of rough across the ridge to the left, but either way the approach is difficult to judge because the green has little depth and the ground at the front tends to gather the ball into the bunkers.

No. 5 564 Yards, Par 5

A group of seven bunkers threaten the drive on the right edge of the fairway, and there are also bunkers set into the hill in front of the green. Against the wind the wise move is to lay-up with the second stroke and play a sound third for a comfortable par.

No. 6 416 Yards, Par 4

There is a blind tee shot with whins left and right, and there is a deep hollow in front of the green which will capture all but the most accurate approach shots. It defines the perfect formula for St Andrews — accuracy from the tee and judgement with the second shot.

No. 7 372 Yards, Par 4

This is the start of the famous Loop of six holes over which scores are either made or marred. The aggressive line from the tee is to the righthand side although there are whins and bushes in the landing area, with pot bunkers and large slopes to protect the front of the green.

No. 8 178 Yards, Par 3

Depending on wind strength and direction, this can require anything from a two iron to a nine iron from the tee, but again good club selection and a tendency to be long is the best strategy to avoid the bunkers at the front of the green.

No. 9 356 Yards, Par 4

In a following wind this green is reachable from the tee, but the difficulty is that it is really an extension of the fairway and for those missing the target, the second shot, whether played as a pitch-and-run or a wedge, is extremely hard to judge and often foils a birdie chance.

No. 10 342 Yards, Par 4

If the wind is right, the green is drivable although a hillock in front has to be negotiated, but even judicious strategy from the tee still requires a short approach that must be judged perfectly on this huge green where the centre rather than the flag itself is the wiser choice.

No. 11 172 Yards, Par 3

The green slopes downwards to the front and is shallow and wide with the flagstick invariably placed towards the front, which is protected by bunkers. Therefore, the tee shot must be perfectly placed to allow an uphill putt. Too wide of the target means a frightening putt across the slopes.

No. 12 316 Yards, Par 4

There is a tempting tee shot for the mighty hitters who may feel they can get home. But a less than perfect shot will find the bunkers or the gorse, so that the risk is arguable, particularly to a green that is raised and rather narrow.

No. 13 425 Yards, Par 4

The Coffin Bunker must be avoided from the tee, even though this leaves a longer second shot which should really be played short and allowed to run through the humps and hollows in front of the green and on to the putting surface.

No. 14 567 Yards, Par 5

This is one of the great holes of golf, where risk and reward have to be balanced with caution. The wise route avoids the Beardies then skirts Hell Bunker to set up a safe third to the green with the prospect of a birdie and the consolation of a par.

No. 15 413 Yards, Par 4

The tee shot favours the left side and the approach is longer than it looks, particularly to a green that is narrow from front to back and requires precise placement of the tee shot to provide the best angle of attack.

No. 16 382 Yards, Par 4

The choice: Either hit between the Principle's Nose Bunkers and the out-of-bounds fence to the right, or play left and hit over Wig Bunker to a green that is protected by a sharp slope.

No. 17 461 Yards, Par 4

The tee shot is directed over the sheds to the right to find the centre of the fairway round the corner of the wall. The safe approach is to the right side of the green to allow the ball to run up, then slow to avoid the road behind while keeping the Road Bunker out of play.

No. 18 354 Yards, Par 4

There is a massive target area from the tee and away from the out-of-bounds fence on the right. But the approach must clear the Valley of Sin at the front left corner, beyond which the flagstick is most frequently placed.

A TIMELESS TEST OF GOLF

BY MICHAEL McDONNELL

There is a deeper significance to the pilgrimage which constantly summons the best golfers of each generation back to the stretch of Scottish coastline upon which the game itself began.

This assembly at St Andrews involves more than a narrow assessment of comparative skills to determine the Champion Golfer of the Year because the entire ritual holds wider importance for the royal and ancient pursuit, indeed for the Old Course itself.

What occurs each time is a comprehensive judgement on the game and its progression from the primitive shape and form in which it left St Andrews in the dim and distant past to whatever new and breathtaking peaks of skill and technology it has reached whenever its latest practitioners return for an Open Championship.

Home of the Royal and Ancient Golf Club

Therein lies the enduring importance of the Old Course. It is more than simply a museum piece and sacred shrine which owes its importance to mere historical chance; it is more valued too than a mecca which golf enthusiasts regard as the game's spiritual home and to which all aspire to make at least one visit in their lifetime.

The Old Course has relevance as a championship test that has not been overwhelmed or outdated by any developing skill or technical advance. It remains timeless and therefore offers the original standard by which all progress can be judged. Accordingly, the new heroes of each era know they must present themselves and adapt their impressive modern talents to a game in its original character and in a style it was intended to be played.

Moreover the Old Course demands skills that are otherwise superfluous in the modern game, yet nonetheless demonstrate degrees of inventiveness and character that have always been essential to a truly successful and complete golfer. It is said that seaside golf, with its random and arbitrary bounces and breaks of fortune in which the punishment far outweighs the crime, tests the man as much as his golf.

That doctrine was carved in stone at the Home of Golf where fairness as such was never an intended ingredient but luck, as much as judgement, earns equal reward with no questions asked. It denotes an attitude of mind that even the greatest players have taken time and painful experience to acquire.

Bobby Jones tore up his card in anguish at the High Hole in his first Open because he was totally bemused by the test with which his prodigious talent was expected to cope. Not only was the landscape alien to him, it gave no clues as to direction, and even a seemingly open piece of terrain was invariably sabotaged with unseen and inescapable pot bunkers just large enough, as the essayist Bernard Darwin noted, for 'one angry man and his niblick.'

In essence, therefore, the Old Course demands that the best players of each era acquire the traditional skills of local knowledge and inventive shotmaking if they wish to succeed. With no obvious route from tee to green, the right line may be just a distant spire or flagpole on which to take aim and keep the ball away from the perils. And if the wind switches, then an alternative target must be found.

After the wide-open first hole, the true character of the Old Course begins to unfold.

Curiously enough, the most ancient of golf courses demands a game plan — that most modern of strategies — from which it is ill-advised to deviate. The best ploy is a kind of stepping-stone approach in which the ball is hit to known and predetermined safe areas and then onwards to other zones so that the hazards are taken out of play.

In theory this should of course reduce players, certainly the contenders, to one level if everybody is obliged to hit to the same areas and thereby limit the outcome to a putting contest on those huge greens. Yet there is an enormous skill required in making the adjustment to adhere closely to such a game plan, and weather conditions constantly change so that only those players who can exert the appropriate discipline on themselves and their golf seem to prevail.

That said, the common view in 1960, when Arnold Palmer turned up to play for the first time and in the process revived the fortunes of the championship and much more besides, was that he decided on a different way to play the Old Course. The Palmer way. He simply attacked all the time and never backed away, and he almost won.

There has been no greater tactician in golf than Jack Nicklaus, who won in 1970 and 1978. It is doubtful whether any of his contemporaries ever prepared as thoroughly as he did for a championship. Before one Open, not at St Andrews, spectators assumed he was having trouble with his driving during practice until he explained, 'I was trying to determine what liberties I could take with the rough.' Point taken, but only from Jack.

Yet his first triumph at St Andrews demanded a total departure from the game plan as he risked all and drove the last green to break his deadlock with Doug Sanders in the 18-hole play-off. The ill-fated Sanders disproved the old saying that 'nobody remembers who came second' because on the previous day he had missed a putt on that same green that would have made him outright champion after having played his way through the ranks from the qualifying rounds.

On the face of it, the mercurial genius of Seve Ballesteros should not have flourished — or indeed endured — for four rounds at the Old Course. Naturally enough, it has always been susceptible to momentary flashes of brilliance — the outward 29 by Tony Jacklin in 1970 when he was defending champion was a classic example. But the Old Course always finds a player out over the long haul. No matter how carefully hidden and protected the weakness may be, the cussed Old Lady of St Andrews will tease and expose it some time in 72 holes.

And yet Ballesteros emerged triumphant in the most dramatic circumstances, when for a time on that Sunday afternoon in 1984 it looked as though Tom Watson was striding towards his third successive Open to rank alongside Harry Vardon as the only other winner of six titles. But the American over-shot the 17th green with his approach and finished on the road while the Spaniard birdied the last hole and went on to win by two strokes.

It is always unwise, of course, to write off a champion, but in the intervening 11 years Watson did not win another Open title. Moreover, the renaissance of European professional golf can probably be traced to that moment, because thereafter a new generation of champions began to emerge, so that by the end of the decade the balance of power in world golf had shifted to a more even position.

By the time Nick Faldo marched in triumph along the final fairway in 1990, he and his contemporaries were well-established figures on the world stage, yet he had learned much about the art of playing St Andrews from his close friend and mentor, Gerald Micklem, a former Captain of the Club and Chairman of the Championship Committee, who had hand-written instructions on the best way to play the Old Course and had even listed specific targets and positions on each hole at which to aim depending on weather conditions.

It served the new champion well, although, sadly, Micklem died two years before his protege captured the title at St Andrews. Micklem's own love of the Old Course stemmed from his attempt to qualify for the 1946 Open Championship for which Dick Burton, the 1939 champion, had waited seven years because of the Second World War for his title defence, and then struck his first tee shot out of bounds over the fence on the right.

Years later Micklem recalled how he had partnered Leonard Crawley, a former Walker Cup player and by then a distinguished golf writer, in a practice round for that Open with Bobby Locke and Norman von Nida, and reflected, 'I learned so much from Leonard that day, but most of all I learned to appreciate the subtlety of the Old Course. It is no use getting cross or trying to do too much. Just cut your losses.'

It was a philosophy that worked well enough when Peter Thomson won the 1955 title and was obliged to hit out backwards from the Beardies in the final round because it was the safest escape route from the

Two of the famous landmarks are Hell Bunker (left) and the Principal's Nose.

The 17th, or Road Hole, is one of the most feared golf holes in the world.

No course is so close to a town as the Old Course.

sand. Worse still, he struck his third into a bunker near the green and had to play out backwards again on his way to a double-bogey 7. But then perhaps that incident defines the essential St Andrews — a place where you twice play in the wrong direction because it is the smartest way to become Open champion.

Even Tony Lema's extraordinary win in 1964 at his first attempt — and with less than two practice rounds — was really a tribute to local knowledge, not his own, of course, but that of Tip Anderson, the local caddie who was to become Palmer's regular employee at the Open until Palmer called it a day in 1995. Lema had such accuracy that he could allow Anderson to choose the club and direction while he obliged with flawless execution.

Yet his victory with such apparent ease prompted concern among some members of the Championship Committee, who wondered whether the Old Course had become an anachronism incapable of defending itself from the modern game and that perhaps the time had come for it to be assigned to the Retired List in the manner of Prestwick, over which the first dozen championships had been played but which

The Valley of Sin, to the front left, is the most prominent feature of the Tom Morris green.

ceased Open service in 1925 never to return.

Yet the subsequent advance of automatic watering plus the mandatory use of what was known as the American ball (the 1.68 inch diameter now in common use) actually added to, or at least maintained, the difficulty of the Old Course. In any case the Committee concluded that winning scores did not matter, provided they were produced by the best players of the day. That principle has certainly held firm with Jack Nicklaus winning twice (1970 and 1978), as well as Seve Ballesteros (1984), Nick Faldo (1990) and now John Daly.

It has to be said that no modern architect would conceive a lay-out like that of the Old Course, with shared fairways and double greens, although the playing principles it observes of strategic values and outrageous penalties form the basis of course design all over the world. Indeed what seems to be a wide open course demands more accuracy than perhaps any other championship venue in golf, and despite those huge greens, the pin positions invariably are located in small areas for all four rounds of a championship, thereby adding to the demands for accuracy.

The last word is with Micklem: 'I am not so precise as to insist that the best man wins, but rather that one of the best men wins. And I like to think that the winner has been rewarded because he understands the challenge of St Andrews and its strategic rather than penal qualities. There are Opens. And then there are Opens at St Andrews. That's the difference.'

Golfers for ages have crossed the Swilcan Bridge.

The widest fairways in golf are to be found on the first and 18th holes of the Old Course.

OPENS IN THE WAR YEARS

BY RAYMOND JACOBS

Of all the Open Championships played at St Andrews, those held immediately before and after the Second World War, in 1939 and 1946, were surely exceptional. Each expressed the mood of their times. There was a sense of impending doom in the first instance. The outbreak of hostilities came less than two months after Dick Burton's victory, and the harbingers were everywhere evident in the daily prints. Then, seven long years later, when Sam Snead won, a pervasive gloom suffused the air. Relief and satisfaction that evil forces had at last been vanquished were tempered by the continuing restrictions on normal life imposed by rationing and shortages. Those who did not experience those times personally would find them difficult to understand.

In that tense time of waiting for the war to begin, at the end of a decade of severe industrial depression and mass unemployment, 15,000 spectators attended over the five days that the 1939 championship lasted — two qualifying rounds on Monday and Tuesday for all players, the first and second rounds of the championship proper on Wednesday and Thursday, and the final 36 holes on Friday. The reward for their enthusiasm was the first domestic triumph at St Andrews since James Braid 29 years before.

As Burton, a tall and powerfully constructed Lancastrian, set about beating the burly American Johnny Bulla by two strokes, in the real world the nation's momentum towards war accelerated. Blackout tests had been introduced and evacuation areas discussed, 40,000 kilts were ordered for Highland regiments, a London hotel room cost 12/6d, a Jaguar car £318 and a sea passage from Glasgow to Boston

Dick Burton waited seven years to defend his 1939 Open title.

£21. In vain the Trades Union Congress and the Labour Party pleaded, 'We must not suffer the indignity and sorrow of drifting into a catastrophic war.' Meanwhile, woods and irons could be had for 19/6d each, and advertisements for domestic staff were abundant.

Splendid mileage was generated by Bulla, who confirmed that he was representing a 'drug-store ball' and that, having discovered that his favourite centre-shafted putter was illegal outside the United States, had to buy a new one and change his putting method.

Bulla declared himself probably the only player in the championship to be using a ball worth the equivalent of ninepence in Britain. He said, 'I am under agreement to play with a 45-cent ball against the ordinary price of $1 you pay in America. You can imagine the fun there was when I led the US Open, playing this ball, up to the last 18 holes.' Bulla added that he would revert to the British-size ball (then 1.62 inches in circumference, compared with the trans-Atlantic 1.68-inch version) if the wind against was particularly strong. Bernard Darwin's comment, loftily detached as ever, was 'Whether he played with it in the championship, I know not, but he played uncommonly well with something.' Indeed he did, as Burton and company were about to discover.

South Africa's Bobby Locke was installed as favourite, with Bulla and fellow-American Lawson Little also highly regarded. Domestic hopes rested on Cotton and, bizarre as it may seem now, the 19-year-old Irish amateur, James Bruen. The pre-qualifying rounds certainly upheld these judgements, for Bruen

Johnny Bulla was runner-up in 1939 and 1946.

led Cotton and Little, with Bulla another stroke behind. Locke was nine adrift of Bruen but, of course, the slate had then to be wiped clean and a new start made. Bruen eventually finished equal 13th. Locke's initial 70 and his second-round 75 included 8 and 7 respectively at the long 14th; Little followed 69, 73 with 79, 80 and fell by the wayside. An Argentinian, Martin Pose, then in contention, took 8 at the 17th in the third round, incurring a two-stroke penalty when he grounded his club in the grass beneath the wall beyond the road, then a hazard, despite his caddie's frantic efforts to explain the rule to a non-English speaker.

As was the way in those less intense days, Bulla, although only five strokes behind Burton, the joint leader with Pose, started the last round so early that he was playing the 16th hole as Burton was on the second. Burton was made aware that, with Bulla having finished with a 73 for 292, he needed 72 to win. Helped by a fortuitous 2 at the short 11th — where his downhill putt struck the back of the hole, jumped, and fell in — Burton eventually required two 5s and two 4s to win by one stroke. He sup-

pressed a heart-stopping moment for his supporters by taking a lofted club for his approach to the Tom Morris green instead of the more conventionally safe pitch and run. All was well, and Burton holed from 15 feet for a birdie 3 and a two-stroke victory.

The fortunes of war decreed that Burton would hold the title longer than anyone without, of course, having been able to convert the victory to his financial advantage. In 1946 he finished 12th, but refused to consider himself unlucky. 'I came through the war,' said Burton, who served in the Royal Air Force, 'and that's a lot more than many did who were at St Andrews that day.' The world the survivors returned to was about to be transformed socially. The championship, too, had an innovation and also an echo from its immediate predecessor at St Andrews, but in the aftermath of war it had no less contentious and gloomy elements surrounding it than the Open which closed the tumultuous events of the 1930s.

That summer the Fuel Minister, Emmanuel Shinwell, warned that there was 'not enough coal to get through the winter.' The black market in 'nylons, chocolate, perfume and other scarce goods' was reported to be flourishing. Footballers threatened to strike for a minimum weekly wage of £7. The Jockey Club announced its intention to install photo-finish cameras at all racecourses. An industrial dispute at Dublin's docks jeopardized supplies of rationed foods. A sonorous, and happily focused, editorial in *The Glasgow Herald* did, however, get its priorities and its reservations in perspective.

Recalling that three of the four Opens played over the Old Course between the wars were won by Americans, it continued, 'Our men will clearly have to solve the golfing paradox of keeping their head down and their chin up if they are to redress the balance.' It was not to be, as indeed it was not until Nick Faldo's 1990 victory. By four strokes Snead gained his only triumph in either the British or American Opens in what was the second of only three appearances. Moreover, Bulla, second on his own in 1939, was again runner-up, a position he shared this time with Locke.

The qualifying rounds were led by Australian Norman von Nida, with Snead and Locke also in the vanguard. John Panton, then the 29-year-old Pitlochry assistant and now the R and A's honorary professional, was disqualified after he reported himself for having practice-putted on one of the New Course greens on the evening before he was due to play there. That episode read as a sort of premonition for the anti-climactic fate which awaited Cotton, after two rounds the leader over Snead by one stroke, with Dai Rees a stroke behind the American, and Bulla and Locke a further stroke in arrears of him. The final-day crowd of some 12,000 — for the first time excluded from the playing area — were again denied the fulfilment of a British success.

It all ended in tears. Cotton walked off the last green of his final round 'and put his head in his hands in disappointment,' having missed a putt of no more than two feet. Not that the lapse would have made any difference, for having closed with rounds of 76, 79, he finished five strokes behind Snead. So, too, did Rees, coming to the home green soon afterwards 'no longer the jaunty, quick-stepping and confident golfer' he had been after his second round of 67, two strokes lower than Locke's opening score. Ironically, the first hole, then of 374 yards and offering the most capacious opening challenge from the tee of any in championship golf, proved to be the start of the downfall of both these British challengers.

Cotton hit his approach into the Swilcan Burn to begin 5, 5, 4, 5, 6 (four over par) and took 40 to reach the turn. Then Rees cut his first drive so badly that it would have gone out of bounds had the ball not struck a spectator. Still, like Cotton, Rees' second fell into the Burn, and with three putts he had started with 7, three over par. Three putts again at the second and third, where his second shots through the wind were not as accurate as before, and Rees sickeningly was 42 to the turn — and out. Rees' last shot of any brilliance came at the 17th, far too late, where he almost holed his second shot. The Road Hole, then 446 yards long, was adjudged a par 5 and Rees' eagle enabled him to finish equal fourth with von Nida, Cotton and Charlie Ward.

Locke, his celebrated putting stroke suddenly so fragile that he was 'only one under 5s for the last six

Sam Snead won his only Open title in 1946.

holes' had to be content with 76 to share second place with Bulla, also round in 79; but even Snead was not immune from potential disaster. At the long fifth his violently hooked drive landed in the 14th's Hell Bunker, his second was in a bush, his third was in another bunker, and his fourth on the edge of the green, whence he was down in two 'for a great 6,' as he later described it. That save secured, Snead was still out in 40 and the turning point, in his judgement, was the birdie 3 he made at the 10th. He then had a fine run home in 35 and could have taken 7 at the last and won.

Not often held up as an example of graciousness even when visiting a country burdened by post-war restrictions, Snead notoriously described playing anywhere outside the United States as 'camping out.' He was not even in time for the prize-giving ceremony, at which Cotton wrily expressed the hope that once British competitors had eaten more good steaks they would have the stomach to finish the course. Snead, it transpired, had gone for a bath, but his West Virginian wise-cracking speech of thanks earned an ovation.

With a wedge shot to eight feet and a birdie putt, Tom Watson was off to 31 on the inward nine for his 67.

AMERICANS SHOW THE WAY

BY ROBERT SOMMERS

As his train chugged into St Andrews spewing smoke and cinders a few days before the 1946 Open Championship, Sam Snead slumped in his seat and sank into a sour mood.

First of all, he hadn't wanted to come to Scotland, but he had been coerced into entering by I.C. Icely, president of the Wilson Sporting Goods Company, which paid him handsomely for playing its clubs. Simply put, Snead had no choice. Then, once he began his trip, everything went wrong.

Trouble began in the New York airport. Sam had taken his seat in the propeller-driven Constellation York while the pilot warmed up the engines. Suddenly fire spouted from one of the engines and the pilot called for everyone to evacuate the aeroplane. Snead and the rest of the passengers scrambled for their lives. Never a grammarian, Snead described the scene by saying, 'Us passengers popped out of that plane like ants.'

Arriving finally in London, Sam couldn't find a room because so many of the hotels had been destroyed by wartime bombing. He solved that problem by catching a short nap on a bench while he waited for the train north.

Then, peering through the carriage windows as the train laboured over from Leuchars, Sam saw what looked to him like the remnants of a few bunkers in a field of unkempt grass and asked, apparently innocently, 'What's that over there? It looks like an old abandoned golf course.'

It was, of course, the Old Course, where the world's oldest golf championship was to begin in a few days, and where Sam would distinguish himself as a successor to Walter Hagen, Gene Sarazen, Denny Shute and Bobby Jones as American winners of the Open.

Times have changed. Hardly anyone would describe the Old Course in quite those terms any longer, for today it is beyond dispute the world's best known golfing ground, so popular and so heavily played

that patrons were handed little patches of carpet to play from early in the year so the fairways could be saved for the 1995 Open Championship.

Snead, by the way, stands among the greatest players of any age. He won that 1946 Open, the first after the Second World War, by shooting 290 and beating Johnny Bulla, a fellow American, and Bobby Locke, the South African who would win four in the future, by four strokes.

Only a few other Americans came to St Andrews that year — Lawson Little and Joe Kirkwood, an Australian by birth, claimed two of the next seven places — but they have come in higher numbers ever since, particularly when the Open has been played at St Andrews, for something about the town and the Old Course draws them like the Lorelei of myth, although not always to their doom.

In the eight Opens that had been played at St Andrews between Snead's victory and 1990, three had been won by American golfers. Tony Lema won in 1964, and Jack Nicklaus won in both 1970 and 1978. Severiano Ballesteros, from Spain, won in 1984 when Tom Watson hit one shot into the gorse on the 12th hole and another into the road on the 17th, and Nick Faldo, from England, won with a dazzling display of precision golf in 1990.

Then, in 1995, when the entries were in, the qualifying done and the final field assembled, its make-up held a surprising figure. Of the 159 who were to start, 55 were Americans, better than one third of the total and actually three more than the total number of British golfers. It could have been more, but five others who were exempt from qualifying withdrew for various reasons — Fred Couples and Fuzzy Zoeller, for example, because of painful backs, and Tom Lehman because his wife had delivered a baby.

Some of those Americans who did play were old and treasured Open hands, principally among them Arnold Palmer, who resuscitated the championship

Ben Crenshaw (67) was in his fourth St Andrews Open.

back in 1960, and Nicklaus, the winner of two St Andrews Opens. Although neither was expected to play a significant part in the outcome, they always add substance to any golf event simply by being there.

Sixty-five years old, Palmer had come to pay a farewell to the Open, which he had come so close to winning in his first attempt, in 1960, and then followed up by taking the next two, at Royal Birkdale in 1961 and at Royal Troon in 1962.

Nicklaus had played his first Open in 1962, shortly after he had beaten Palmer in a play-off for the US Open, but he scored 10 on the 11th, the Railway Hole, and missed the 36-hole cut. Later, of course, he won three Opens, his first at Muirfield, in 1966, and then his two at St Andrews.

Other Americans presented genuine threats, though. No golfer is more appreciated by the Scots than Watson, the winner of five Open Championships, four of them in Scotland, and no one is appreciated by more golf fans anywhere than Ben Crenshaw, who has yet to win one. Both of them were playing in their fourth St Andrews Opens, and even though each man was in his 40s, they had shown signs they could still compete. Watson, for example, had played very well at Turnberry in 1994, and Crenshaw had won the Masters in April. Then, in the opening round, they delighted their fans with some wonderful golf.

Each man shot 67, five strokes under the course par, the best score of the field. When the round ended in the twilight of a long day, they were tied with John Daly, another American, and Mark McNulty, from Zimbabwe.

The opening round of any big occasion usually generates moments of surprise, now and then reviving memories of the past and glimpses of the future. Opening day in 1995 had a few of those moments. Besides the low scores of the leaders, we saw disappointing moments as well — Nicklaus, for example, taking another 10, this one on the 14th after four miserable shots from Hell Bunker, and Palmer needing 83 frustrating strokes to work his way around. With 78, Nicklaus beat only four other golfers, and Palmer came in dead last.

Mark McNulty (67) made four birdies in the Loop.

John Daly (67) used his driver on all but two holes.

At 7.10 Pedro Linhart of Spain hit the first tee shot of the 124th Open Championship.

Those high scores, however, were exceptions, for only occasionally in the past had the Old Course been battered so badly as it was on this day. When darkness fell, 59 players had broken its par of 72, another 25 had matched it, and only 75 had shot 73 or higher. Considering what lay ahead, these were strange figures indeed.

Moistened by early morning fogs, the fairways looked lush and green, but their appearance masked hard, fast-running ground that had taken only scattered rains for the previous six to eight weeks. Though the greens were not particularly fast, they would be firm and hard to hold, as they should be for a championship.

Still, five years earlier the 1990 championship had confirmed that the Old Course needs weather to stiffen its defences. Under the mild and warm condi-

tions of that week, scoring had dropped to alarming levels. At the height of his powers then, Faldo had shot 67 and 65 in the first two rounds, and Greg Norman had kept up with two rounds of 66, which matched the record 67-65 of Henry Cotton in the unforgettable 1934 Open at Sandwich. Then, as the early starters of 1995 began testing the Old Course, it began to look as if we might see 1990 repeated. Russell Claydon, the big, former English Amateur champion, dipped to three under par after seven holes; the American Jim Gallagher played the first nine in three under par, and Corey Pavin, the US Open champion, stood three under par after 12 holes. Both Pavin and Gallagher held on and shot 69s, and Claydon finished with 70.

A breeze had begun rising early on the morning of the opening round, blowing at a steady 10 to 15

Bill Glasson (68) blasted from the Lion's Mouth Bunker before the 13th green and saved par.

David Feherty (68) was again off to a good start.

Vijay Singh (68) three-putted the 10th from 50 feet.

miles an hour at first, with gusts to 20, but we needed a stronger wind.

Even though Watson had said he preferred a windy day because it creates another hazard, he struggled to hold his own through the first nine, and indeed played shaky golf on the opening hole. A much better driver of the ball than he had been in his youth, Watson nevertheless pulled his first tee shot so far left he must have been more than 100 yards from Norman, whose own drive stopped only a couple yards short of tumbling into the Swilcan Burn, where it runs parallel to the fairway before crossing in front of the green. Then he pushed his seven-iron approach so far right he left himself a putt of fully 70 feet. Then he holed it. As the putt dropped he grinned and raised his arms aloft as if he had won the championship.

With the wind coming in slightly south of west, crossing from left to right and partially into the golfer's face, Tom played an uneasy opening nine holes in 36 after losing a stroke on the eighth, the par 3.

Turning around then, with the wind right to left and slightly behind, Watson sped home in 31 by playing marvellous golf. Some of his shots were wonderful to watch, particularly his seconds to the 13th and 14th. By then he had birdied both the 10th and

Mats Hallberg (68) finished par, birdie.

31

Per-Ulrik Johansson (69) went out in 32.

12th with wedge approaches to eight and six feet. A three wood played to a safe position short of the hill rising before the 13th green left him another seven-iron approach. He hit it hard, aiming to a point perhaps 30 yards right of the flagstick, set in a difficult position about 15 feet from the green's right edge. The ball shot off on line, curled back and came at the green almost sideways, hit, and settled perhaps four feet from the cup. Always ready to applaud genius, the largely Scottish gallery roared. Watson looked toward them with his usual tight-lipped smile, and holed the putt. On to the 14th, the 567-yard par 5.

Where both Norman and amateur Gordon Sherry took the safer route, driving to the left of the Beardies and playing it as a true three-shot hole, Watson drove straight ahead to the Elysian Fields, played a three wood for his second that soared outside the stone wall defining out of bounds along the right, and once again turned his ball back on to the green, stopping it perhaps 15 feet from the flag. He holed the putt for an eagle 3.

Four under par now, Watson holed from four feet to save par on the 16th and got down in two from 25 feet on the 17th. Safely past the most dangerous parts of the course, and with the wind more nearly at his back now, Tom drove left of the final green so close he putted within 10 feet of the hole, then ran it in.

As Watson, Norman and Sherry strode up the 18th fairway, they saw Palmer ready to begin his round. Arnold leaned on his driver and watched them finish.

Tom's score stood through a good portion of the round, until the wind slackened late in the afternoon. Play had been painfully slow, with rounds taking as much as five hours, principally because of how the professionals play the Old Course, crisscrossing fairways and waiting while other groups putted on the huge double greens.

McNulty was the second to post his 67, which was perhaps the major surprise of the day, for a month earlier he had been playing terrible stuff after changing his swing. His game had grown only worse, so bad he had missed more cuts than he had made, seven in succession on the American Tour, and so he went into consultation with David Leadbetter, his life-long friend and teacher. The results were startling.

Off just after noon, McNulty stood at even par when he came to the Loop, the swing of holes at the far end of the course, then reeled off four consecutive birdies on the seventh through the 10th with exceptional iron play and sound putting. He played a sand wedge to eight feet on the seventh, a five iron to 18 feet on the eighth, another sand wedge to six inches on the ninth and an eight iron to 12 feet on the 10th.

After another birdie on the 14th, where he reached the green with a three wood for his second and two-putted from 20 feet, McNulty cringed as his five-iron approach trickled off the 17th green and on to the road. From a rough lie on the tarmac he ran the ball up the bank and on to the green, then holed from 15 feet to save his par.

Surprisingly, considering his background, Daly had built up an enthusiastic following in Britain, principally because of his mammoth driving, but just as well perhaps because of his exceptional touch around the greens, as he had demonstrated here in the 1993 Alfred Dunhill Cup. It had been obvious from the time he won the 1991 USPGA Championship that he could play those little chips and pitches that often save a round. Although he has a tendency toward impatience, he seemed completely under control as the Open began, perhaps because he ran off three quick birdies beginning with the third. He made his first two by holing putts from the reasonable distance of eight feet, but his last, on the fifth, took his breath away. He covered the 567 yards from the tee to the green with a driver and a three iron, but the second shot left him 41 paces from the cup. ('I know it was 41 paces because I walked it off,' he said.) In danger of three-putting, Daly coaxed his first putt within five feet, then holed it.

Even with another birdie on the ninth, his fourth of the day, Daly went out in 34 because of two bogeys, but he came back with three more birdies, making seven in all. He made his last on the home hole under rather unusual circumstances. As everyone else does, Daly played his drive to the left, but when he pulled it, the ball rolled on and on and eventually ran into

David Duval (71) took 7 on the Road Hole.

the gallery beyond the metal fencing that kept the spectators in check. After a free drop back on the course, Daly played a neat little running shot that pulled up within seven feet of the cup and holed it for an incoming 33 and a 67 that impressed even himself.

Settling down after the round, Daly said, 'I think that's the most patient golf I've ever played. Certainly it's the best I've hit the ball since I don't know when, and I had more birdies today than I've had all season.'

Crenshaw, too, played better than he had in some time, racing out in 33 with three birdies, and home in 34. One of the great putters of his generation, Ben holed only one putt of any length, running in a 20-footer on the fifth and another from 12 feet on the 15th, which sometimes seems commonplace for him. He showed a weakness that would turn up later when he three-putted the fourth. Ben played what may have been his best shot of the day on the 17th, a sweeping hook with a two iron that ran to the heart of the green. It earned him no more than a par 4, but only two men did better that day, and 75 scored higher.

Not everyone, though, could bask in the glow of a successful opening, although several others played especially well. David Feherty, who finished tied for fourth at Turnberry in 1994, shot 68, along with

Greg Norman (71) played despite a sore back.

Nick Price (70) said he made several mental errors.

Jack Nicklaus (78) made 10 from Hell Bunker.

Seve Ballesteros (75) had a frustrating start.

Vijay Singh, Bill Glasson and Mats Hallberg. A young American, David Duval, was looking to join them until he took 7 on the 17th and finished with 71. It was the first of eight scores of 7 or worse on the Road Hole during the championship.

Pavin shot 69 and left himself in good position, and defending champion Nick Price, who seemed edgy after his great year in 1994, shot an erratic 70, combining six birdies with four bogeys.

At the same time Norman kept himself in position with 71 after wondering if his tender back would keep him from playing at all.

Faldo, though, shot 74 on a day when he could neither drive nor putt. Time after time he would hit the ball and follow its flight as if he were in pain. He summed up his day nicely when he said, 'I just didn't make anything out of anything.'

Jim Gallagher Jnr (69) eagled the 18th hole.

Steve Lowery (69) birdied the Road Hole.

Darren Clarke (69) overcame four bogeys.

FIRST ROUND RESULTS

HOLE	1	2	3	4	5	6	7	8	9	10	11	12	13	14	15	16	17	18	
PAR	3	4	4	4	5	4	4	3	4	4	3	4	4	5	4	4	4	4	TOTAL
Tom Watson	3	4	4	4	5	4	4	4	4	3	4	3	3	3	4	4	4	3	67
Mark McNulty	4	3	4	4	6	4	3	2	3	3	3	4	4	4	4	4	4	4	67
John Daly	4	4	3	3	4	5	4	4	3	4	3	3	4	4	4	4	4	3	67
Ben Crenshaw	4	3	4	5	4	3	3	3	4	4	3	4	4	4	3	4	4	4	67
David Feherty	3	5	3	4	4	5	3	3	4	4	2	4	4	4	4	4	4	4	68
Vijay Singh	4	3	4	4	5	4	3	3	4	5	3	4	4	4	4	4	4	3	68
Bill Glasson	4	4	4	4	5	4	3	3	3	4	4	4	4	4	3	4	4	3	68
Mats Hallberg	4	4	3	4	5	5	4	3	4	4	3	3	4	3	4	4	4	3	68
Corey Pavin	4	4	3	5	4	4	3	3	4	4	3	3	4	4	4	4	5	4	69
Jim Gallagher Jnr	4	4	4	4	4	4	3	3	3	4	4	5	5	4	3	5	4	2	69
Steve Lowery	4	4	4	4	4	4	3	3	3	4	3	3	5	5	4	5	3	4	69
Darren Clarke	4	4	3	3	5	5	5	3	3	3	3	5	4	3	4	5	4	3	69
David Gilford	4	4	4	4	5	4	3	3	4	4	2	4	3	5	4	4	4	4	69
Gene Sauers	3	4	4	4	5	4	4	3	4	4	3	4	4	4	4	4	4	3	69
Costantino Rocca	3	5	4	4	4	4	4	2	4	3	2	5	5	5	3	4	4	4	69
John Cook	4	4	4	4	5	3	3	3	4	2	3	5	5	3	4	5	4	4	69
Per-Ulrik Johansson	4	3	4	4	4	4	3	3	3	4	4	4	5	5	4	3	4	4	69

HOLE SUMMARY

HOLE	PAR	EAGLES	BIRDIES	PARS	BOGEYS	HIGHER	RANK	AVERAGE
1	4	0	32	108	18	1	13	3.92
2	4	0	17	101	34	7	5	4.20
3	4	0	44	108	7	0	16	3.77
4	4	0	10	116	33	0	7	4.14
5	5	1	65	75	15	3	16	4.71
6	4	0	12	94	51	2	3	4.27
7	4	0	30	105	23	1	11	3.97
8	3	0	16	111	32	0	8	3.10
9	4	0	28	119	12	0	14	3.90
OUT	36	1	254	937	225	14		35.98
10	4	0	24	121	13	1	12	3.94
11	3	0	12	109	36	2	4	3.18
12	4	0	23	116	18	2	9	3.99
13	4	0	7	87	57	8	2	4.43
14	5	3	53	86	15	2	15	4.77
15	4	0	20	123	15	1	10	3.98
16	4	0	12	112	34	1	6	4.15
17	4	0	2	82	64	11	1	4.53
18	4	1	47	101	10	0	18	3.75
IN	36	4	200	937	262	28		36.72
TOTAL	72	5	454	1874	487	42		72.70

			LOW SCORES		
Players Below Par	59				
Players At Par	25		Low First Nine	Per-Ulrik Johansson	32
Players Above Par	75			Frank Nobilo	32
			Low Second Nine	Tom Watson	31
			Low Round	Ben Crenshaw	67
				John Daly	67
				Mark McNulty	67
				Tom Watson	67

Television personnel, photographers and journalists closely followed the Open Championship.

Gordon Sherry impressed many including Tom Watson, who said Sherry had 'a great sense of humour and he can play.'

COMMENTARY

THE TOAST OF THE OPEN

BY MICHAEL WILLIAMS

From his ginger hair to his height of 6-foot-8 and 18 stone Gordon Sherry stands out in any crowd. But for a young man of those proportions, you would expect to see him in the line-out for Scotland at Murrayfield rather than on the first tee at St Andrews in an Open Championship.

Big men like that are supposed to be at a disadvantage at golf. Even Nick Faldo, who is five inches shorter, has wished in the past that he could lose another three or four. Andy North, even though he did win two US Open Championships — but not much else — must also have speculated as to how better he might have been if he had not stood at 6-foot-4 in his stocking feet. So, too, Peter Oosterhuis, 6-foot-5, who once in the early 1970s held a three-stroke lead going into the last round of the Masters only to drop it because he could not keep out of the trees.

It would be premature to predict exactly what golfing heights Sherry will achieve, but for a 21-year-old student at Stirling University he does appear to possess one priceless asset. Call it luck, call it what you will, he is a man to whom things seem to 'happen.'

So far as the amateurs were concerned, all the expectation and curiosity in these two weeks in Scotland, with first the Scottish Open at Carnoustie and then the Open itself at golf's headquarters, belonged to Tiger Woods, the American Amateur champion who from a tender age, and still only 19, has been lauded as the latest — and there have been a few — best prospect since Jack Nicklaus.

Yet even though Woods, on his first appearance in Britain, completed all four rounds in both the Scottish and the Open, it is only a slight exaggeration to say that he was eclipsed, overshadowed in every respect as he was by Sherry and that boyish grin of his.

Sherry came to national, as opposed to Scottish,

prominence in 1994 when the Amateur Championship broke new ground at Nairn, which is almost as far north as Dornoch and in 1999 will stage the Walker Cup. He got to the final where he was beaten by Lee James, an Englishman.

Because of his very bulk there were those of us who suspected that this was just a 'flash in the pan,' but 12 months later, in the 100th Amateur at Hoylake, where it had all begun in 1885, Sherry again got to the final and this time beat, which is about the politest term for it, Michael Reynard by 7 and 6.

It was not however in the final that Sherry particularly impressed so much as in the earlier rounds when on three occasions he was very much under the whip coming down the home straight and once, against David Howell, who was also selected for the Walker Cup at Royal Porthcawl in the autumn, seemingly on his way home when 3 down with six holes to play. Indeed even Sherry afterwards admitted to be thinking more of the long drive home up the M6 to Scotland than he was of being in the next round.

But, over that testing finish when the wind was stiff from the west, Sherry's game went up a gear each time, his play of the 17th, where there is an out-of-bounds fence just behind the green, being quite superb as he struck a series of plumb drives and longish irons right on target.

It was highly impressive stuff, and so, too, were Sherry's performances the following month when he was the battering ram in Scotland's victory in the European Amateur Team Championship at Royal Antwerp when they defeated England by 6-1 in the final. Sherry won his every match.

That was a demanding week for him, what with all the practice rounds, the two qualifying rounds and then the match-play stages, and Sherry admitted to being 'on his knees' by the time he arrived at Carnoustie where he began the Scottish Open with 73.

Sherry displayed a great touch round the Old Course and was not awed by the occasion.

What happened after that was quite outstanding as Sherry, armed with a new driver that he had hit only 10 times in the practice ground, went on to record rounds of 70, 71 and 69 for a total of 283, seven strokes behind the winner, Wayne Riley, of Australia, but good enough for a tie for fourth place with another Australian, Craig Parry. It was the best performance by an amateur in a PGA European Tour event, and the birdie he got at the 18th in the last round fairly raised the roof with a Scottish following that had taken him to their hearts.

As Amateur champion, Sherry did not have to qualify for the Open at St Andrews, but the spotlight was now well and truly on him, especially when the draw came out for the first round with him in the same threeball as Greg Norman and Tom Watson. In practice he also made the 'big time,' when he was invited to join Watson, Nicklaus and Tom Wargo, who the previous year had won the British Seniors Open at Royal Lytham.

It was then that Sherry must have realized that he had been born under a lucky star, for if that company was not enough in itself, he also had the great fortune to have a hole-in-one at the eighth. 'It was my dream really,' said Sherry afterwards. 'It was only my second hole-in-one. It was 158 yards and I hit a seven iron. I could not see it go in but I could hear the cheers.'

Of this practice round, Sherry said it had been 'fun.' Both Nicklaus and Watson had offered to be of any help they could. 'I just talked to them about university,' where in the autumn he would be entering his third year in his quest for a degree in biochemistry. Unlike too many young players these days, he is in no rush to turn professional, sensibly recognizing the need for a second string to his bow.

Watson told him that he would take him round Augusta for a practice round before the Masters, while 'Jack said that if I wanted to come to the Memorial (at Muirfield Village in 1996), the invitation was there. I said I would be there and he said my exams must come first. I said I could still be there!'

Nicklaus did not pass comment on Sherry's game. 'You don't want to change things the day before you play in the Open,' Sherry said. 'Jack still hits it a long way and so does Tom. He hits it miles. Wargo is a bit shorter but not that short. Maybe I was a bit longer but it depended on what kicks I got. I suppose I hit it about 280 to 290.'

As this practice round did not matter, Sherry was quite relaxed. Having killed his opening drive down the first fairway, he thought of the 20 major championships Nicklaus had won and the eight of Watson. The nerves, he knew, were still to come.

Afterwards Sherry went off to think about his 'game plan' for his first round and what he was going to hit off every tee. He suspected some tough pin positions, particularly if the weather was calm. 'Otherwise someone will kill the course,' he guessed.

It was inevitable that he should be thinking about

turning professional, but he was determined that he will get his final year at university out of the way first. 'If you think I have locked myself away for 10 hours a day for weeks on end and am then going to throw it all away, there's no chance. I know I have the ability to play good golf, so with another year's practice and a year's maturity, I shall be right up there,' he said.

Off early in the first round, Sherry rose at six o'clock and, like many a student on campus, promptly 'threw up.' It was not, however, too much to drink that was the cause, or even nerves. He had eaten something which disagreed with him the night before when dining locally with his parents. But he had slept well. 'Of course I slept well,' he retorted. 'All students sleep well.'

There had been some doubt as to whether Norman would be on the tee. He had revealed on the eve of the championship that he had been suffering from a bad back and had managed only one practice round. He made his decision to play only after hitting some shots on the range before teeing off.

Nonetheless, Norman no longer had the short price on his head he would have done if he had been fully fit, but it was still a great effort by Sherry to have the better score, 70 to 71, as Watson beat them both with 67.

Watson was impressed. 'What a delightful guy to play with,' he commented afterwards. 'He has a good rhythm and a great arc to his swing. He can play. Heck, he could play rugby, too.'

Norman would agree with that. There was one occasion when the Australian threw his ball to his caddie for cleaning. Sherry happened to be standing between them and Norman laughed when he said that he had never had to flip the ball so high to avoid an interception, like a hooker trying to avoid the big man in the middle to find his target at the far end of the line-out.

Perhaps the worst thing for Sherry was the length of time it took to play 18 holes, just about five and a half hours, though this was not the longest in his experience. In the Eisenhower Trophy in Paris in 1994, he was on the course for six hours. The worst wait was at the fourth and fifth holes. 'It felt like half

Sherry became a gallery favourite.

an hour,' he said, 'and I had to steady myself.' It may have had something to do with his dropping a shot at the fourth, but with birdies at the third and ninth, where he drove the green and then two-putted, he was out in 35.

He was through the green at the 11th and in a gorse bush at the 12th, each time to drop shots. With the wind at his back, he was too big with a seven-iron second shot to the 567-yard 14th, but slotted a long putt for his birdie at the 15th, scraped his pars at the 16th and 17th, and then finished with a 3 driving into the Valley of Sin and getting down in two putts.

Thus was a star born and it continued to twinkle in the second round when Sherry followed with 71 to be three under par and on the leaderboard, ahead still not only of Norman but now as well Watson, who had subsided. With Tiger Woods eclipsed, the silver medal as leading amateur seemed to be Sherry's for the taking, and it was a disappointment to the Scots that Steven Webster, who is about half Sherry's size and, to make matters worse, English, nipped through to beat him.

In the long term, however, it is likely to be Sherry who will make the bigger mark. As he eventually found his way through the last of the autograph hunters and sank into the back seat of his courtesy car, an admiring young driver, trying to conceal a mild flush, murmured: 'He's wonderful, just wonderful. And his eyes speak, too.'

Co-leader Brad Faxon (138) had never played the Old Course before, but felt he knew it from watching on television.

A PIVOTAL ROUND FOR DALY

BY ROBERT SOMMERS

Midway through the second round at Turnberry last year, John Daly had worked himself into position where he might lead at the halfway point. He had opened with 68 and followed with some inspired golf on the outward nine of the second round. Three birdies had dropped him to five under par for 27 holes. He had gone out in 32, but his score might have been better had he taken advantage of some other opportunities; he had missed a number of putts from inside 15 feet that could have dropped his score into the 20s had they fallen.

Every golfer knows, though, that one misplayed shot may lead to ruin. It happened to Daly as suddenly his game collapsed and he didn't know how to handle it. From the 10th tee he played a terrible hook that dived among the rocks along the shoreline of the Clyde estuary and disappeared. He made 7 there and followed up by four-putting the 11th — five strokes lost in two holes. He was never the

Former US President George Bush, a member of the R and A, and his wife attended the Open.

same, eventually shot a petulant 80 in the last round and finished last among those who played all 72 holes.

Thoughts of that moment flashed through the mind as Daly pushed his drive into the cluster of bunkers set to the right of the fifth fairway, the first of the two par-5 holes of the Old Course during the second round of the 1995 Open Championship. Daly could reach this green with his second shot and pick up another birdie, but now that opportunity was gone. Soon any thoughts of a par had flown as well. John struggled out, pitched back to the fairway, and took two more shots to reach the green. He scored a 7, dropping two strokes.

His gallery held its breath, because one mistake like this could have ruined him in the past. But this was a more mature Daly. Surprising everyone, he brushed it off and went back to work, played the next four holes of the outward nine in pars, then birdied four of the next five and came back in 33, shot 71 for the day, and when the round ended still held a share of the lead at 138, six strokes under par.

With Daly's resilience ranked among its high points, this was a pivotal day in the championship, a day when Brad Faxon and Katsuyoshi Tomori rose to join Daly at the top, when Tom Watson and Mark McNulty began falling back, when Costantino Rocca hinted he might be around for a while, when Ben Crenshaw hung on by his fingertips, when Ernie Els might have moved ahead and yet blundered on the late holes, when Nick Faldo thrust himself back into the championship with a stirring 67, when Nick Price confirmed that he would not defend his championship successfully by shooting 74, and when Arnold Palmer played his last strokes in the Open Championship.

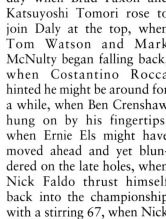

It was, furthermore, a day that saw the field so closely bunched that 103 golfers completed 36 holes within 10 strokes of one another and survived the halfway cut. Furthermore, while Faxon, Tomori and Daly had risen to the top, they were being pressed by six others just one stroke behind, and three more just two behind. Some of those were among the most dangerous players in the game. Crenshaw, who dreams of winning the Open, had slipped from 67 to 72, but at 139 he stood at five under par, along with

John Daly (138) drove the 18th green, then three-putted from 45 feet for par.

Katsuyoshi Tomori (138) had his caddie point the lines.

Corey Pavin, one of the game's better wind players; Els, the 1994 US Open champion; Mark Brooks, another American, and Rocca, a likeable 38-year-old Italian who had placed second in two tournaments earlier in the season.

It was a day for amateurs as well. Grouped with Watson and Greg Norman, Gordon Sherry outplayed them both by shooting 71 — taking his drive on the 17th over the roof of the Old Course Hotel — and Steven Webster nearly stealing the lead with a first nine of 32, but then stumbling home in 40. Webster had nearly holed his second shot to the fifth, hitting a 265-yard three wood within two feet of the hole, and when he followed with a birdie 3 on the seventh after a sand wedge to four feet, he stood six under par. A run of four consecutive bogeys coming home ruined him, and he fell into a tie for 20th at 142, one stroke behind Sherry.

The wind had strengthened overnight and whipped in from the southwest once again at a force approaching 30 miles an hour late in the day, which made some of the more imaginative hole locations quite difficult to reach. The freshening breeze not only flung high-flying shots about, but it had the further effect of blowing putts off line and drying out the greens as well. By day's end they had become quite firm and often difficult to hold with a pitch. It was a day for low, running approach shots, the genius of links golf.

Costantino Rocca (139) felt he knew the course.

Mark Brooks (139) had six birdies and three bogeys.

Surprisingly, Watson, whom everyone knows as one of the game's best bad weather players — How else could he have won five Opens? — evidently couldn't handle the conditions and slipped to 76, even though he birdied four holes. His round was destroyed, though, by double-bogey 6s on the first, ninth and 17th holes. Losing two strokes on both the fifth and the 17th, McNulty shot 76 as well, and at 143 fell from first to 31st, along with Watson, Bernhard Langer, David Feherty, who had played so well at Turnberry, Mark Calcavecchia, the last American to win the Open, and Ken Green. Green, incidentally, had been involved in a somewhat bizarre incident. Among them, Green, Hisayuki Sasaki and Jose Rivero completed the 12th in only eight strokes. Green and Sasaki both scored eagle 2s while Rivero could only par. Sasaki shot 71, Green and Rivero 72.

Strangely enough for a player distinguished by thundering, high-flying drives, Daly had shown an aptitude for the type of golf conditions the Old Course demands during the 1993 Alfred Dunhill Cup, played in chilly weather in the autumn. That had been his introduction to the Old Course, and he found he liked it. Bumping approaches on to the rolling, tumbling greens, he won four of his five matches and led the United States to victory.

While he hadn't returned since then, he picked up his touch right away, and, furthermore, found he could use his best-known weapon more often than he thought he might. His practice rounds showed him he could play his driver on all the par-4 and -5 holes except the 12th, a 316-yard par 4 he could reach with his one iron.

Of course when he ripped into his one iron on Friday, it was difficult to agree on whether he hit the green because his ball settled almost 200 feet from the cup. He was, in fact, closer to the hole of the sixth than of the 12th. But Daly has an amazing touch. He lagged his first putt within five feet of the cup and holed it for a birdie 3. Exaggerating, of course, he said this was the hardest he had hit a ball all day.

By then he had birdied both the 10th and 11th, making up the strokes he had lost on the fifth, and now he stood at one under par. He lost the stroke by three-putting the 13th, perhaps through overconfidence, since his approach settled only 50 feet from the hole. His first putt pulled up six feet short and he missed. Quickly, he won it back again on the 14th, where with the wind slightly behind him he showed what his immense power could do. After tearing into his drive, he threw himself into a six iron that rolled within 10 feet of the cup. He two-putted for the birdie. He might have birdied the last as well, but he missed from six feet.

Daly had gone off among the early starters, a little after nine o'clock, but Faxon had been on the course

Ernie Els (139) saw a potential lead melt away.

for more than an hour by then. A lean redhead from Rhode Island who stands a little over six feet tall, Faxon had been in the thick of the 1994 Open and had in fact gone into the last round in a first-place tie with Fuzzy Zoeller, two strokes ahead of Price. A closing 73 dropped him to seventh.

Although he had never played the Old Course before the previous weekend, Faxon felt he knew it because he had seen it so often on television back in the United States. He could still remember Seve Ballesteros winning in 1984, and could even remember the blue and white sweater Nicklaus had worn in 1978.

Faxon loves the kind of test the Old Course lays before you. Since he plays by feel, he believed he had a definite edge because, 'When you're just off the green, you have to make decisions, like whether you

As Tom Watson (143) demonstrated, the drive from the 17th tee presented an unusual challenge.

want to bump it or run it or flick it or lob it. There's no place to practise those things; you have to play by instinct.'

Apparently Faxon's instincts were on target. He played the first nine of the second round in 34, then started the journey home by holing from seven feet on the 10th. He lost a stroke on the 11th by three-putting from 70 feet following a loose six-iron tee shot, but he holed another putt from seven feet on the 12th and once again dropped to three under par for the day.

A driver and a three wood left him at least 100 feet from the hole on the 14th, but showing the touch that makes him one of the game's best putters, Brad coaxed his first putt within two feet and knocked it in. Another birdie; now he stood four under par for the round.

Ben Crenshaw (139) left many approach putts short.

Corey Pavin (139) finished with a 3, driving the 18th.

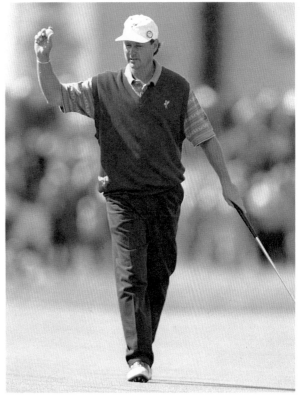

John Cook (139) was happy with his putting.

Amateur Steven Webster (142) took the lead after 25 holes.

Three consecutive pars brought him to the home hole needing one more birdie to reach six under par for two rounds, the same as a year ago. His putt from 10 feet dropped, and he had his 67.

Where both Daly and Faxon claimed a liking for the challenges and techniques of links golf, Tomori wasn't sure if he felt the same. Speaking through an interpreter, the Japanese golfer said his decision would be based on how well he finished. He did say, however, he believed the Old Course was too difficult. He hadn't played as if it were, though. Playing quite steady golf, Tomori went out in 34 with birdies on the fifth, where he reached the green with his second shot, and on the seventh, where he lofted a sand wedge to four feet.

Coming back he birdied three holes, holing from 10 feet on the 12th, reaching the 14th with his second and getting down in two, then rolling in a 25-foot putt on the 16th. He had only one blemish, a bogey 5 on the 13th, where he three-putted from about 100 feet.

Others weren't quite so fortunate. Els had played outstanding golf through the first 14 holes, six under par for the round and seven under for the distance, and had struck some extraordinary shots to get there. He had hit a 60-yard pitch to four feet at the third and almost holed a low, punched eight-iron shot on the 10th. Four holes later he covered the 567 yards of the 14th with a drive and a five iron, chalking up his sixth birdie of the day. Four more pars and he would have 66 and lead the field with 137.

Els found on the 15th that greed often leads to trouble. Left with a pitch of about 115 yards, Ernie tried to play a little wedge with lots of backspin, but he yanked it 40 feet left of the hole and three-putted.

'That was the turning point,' he said later.

Then he nearly saved his par after missing the 17th green, but he missed from four feet and bogeyed again. Instead of 66, he shot 68.

Angry at his finish, Els brushed past reporters and hurried to his hotel. He came back after a cooling shower, admitted he had been 'quite annoyed,' and added, 'I had the opportunity to pull away and maybe pushed too hard. I was playing so well. I got to seven under, and just a couple more birdies ...'

Payne Stewart (140) had 68 to pull within two strokes.

Still, he stuck among the leaders, which was a better position than Bill Glasson's. A blond Californian with knees so bad he often wears callipers, Glasson had begun the day only one stroke off the lead, and by the end of 16 holes stood two under par for the round and six under for 34 holes. Two more pars and he would catch Faxon and Daly, who had already finished. His threat ended there; he made 8 on the par-4 17th without ever going into either the road or the Road Bunker. It would prove to be the highest score there of the week, on the toughest hole of the course. His drive soared out of bounds, into the grounds of the Old Course Hotel, his third shot cleared the hotel grounds and dived into the rough, his fourth found a bunker far short of the green, his fifth was still short, and he three-putted. He finished with 74 and dropped to 142. Instead of a tie for first, he fell into a tie for 20th.

The day also raised what turned out to be false hope for both Faldo and John Cook. Faldo's 67, which matched the best scores of the round, followed his opening 74 and seemed typical of the man, who had so often struck back when he seemed beaten, but it led to nothing except assuring him that he would make the cut for the 20th consecutive year.

Cook had had a grim Open record since his disappointment of 1992, when he nearly won at Muirfield but instead finished second to Faldo. He gave Nick his opening by missing a birdie putt from inside two feet on the 17th, and then bogeyed the last. He missed the cut the following year, then dropped to 55th place at Turnberry in 1994. His opening 69 at St Andrews raised his hopes, and then he shot 70 in the second, a score that could have been better. First-class irons placed him inside 15 feet on every hole on the home nine except the 10th, where he three-putted from 25 feet. He also drove the 12th green and two-putted for a birdie from 50 feet.

Daly's missed putt on the 18th turned out to be a costly miss for the R and A. Had he holed and turned in a 36-hole score of 137, the field for the final two rounds would have been reduced by nine players. At the same time the missed putt meant a reprieve for Jack Nicklaus, who rebounded from his opening 78 with 70 in the second. Since his 148 fell within 10

Bill Glasson (142) had his hopes ruined on the Road Hole.

Justin Leonard (140) equalled the day's low with 67.

Bernhard Langer (143) was just out of contention.

Jose Maria Olazabal (144) had two level-par rounds.

Colin Montgomerie (150) was very disappointed.

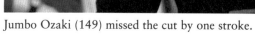

Brian Watts (143) led the Japan Order of Merit.

Jumbo Ozaki (149) missed the cut by one stroke.

Nick Faldo (141) recovered with 67: 'I kept the ball in play and holed some putts. Simple as that.'

strokes of the leader, he had survived the cut and was assured of matching J.H. Taylor's record of 30 appearances on the final day.

One other mighty veteran of the Open qualified without help from the 10-stroke rule. With a round of 73 to go with his opening 71, 59-year-old Gary Player qualified to play the final two rounds for the 26th time in an Open career going back to 1956. The champion in 1959, 1968 and 1974, he is the oldest man to survive the 36-hole cut since the end of the Second World War.

Others, of course, weren't so lucky. Ian Baker-Finch, the 1991 champion, had gone into so deep a slump he hadn't played 72 holes in any of the 13 tournaments he had entered in the United States or his native Australia, and had won absolutely no money. Then, as he played his first drive of the championship, the wind flipped his visor over his eyes in mid-stroke, and he pulled the shot all the way across the double fairway and out of bounds. He shot 77-76–153.

Fighting back from cancer, Paul Azinger would have made the cut if he only had three-putted the home green, but he needed four and missed by one stroke. Colin Montgomerie played badly, posting two rounds of 75; Bob Tway, so close in the US Open, missed by one stroke, along with Curtis Strange, ruined by a second round of 76.

Palmer missed the cut as well, but, nevertheless, the day really belonged to him. He was a triumph, flashing memories of his glory years when he slashed his way around the golf course, alternately hitching his pants and knocking the flagstick from the hole. Those who followed him saw some of the old Palmer fire over the last few holes.

In his day, Palmer was perhaps the best driver in the game; he showed it over those last few holes. Standing on the 16th tee, he looked at the cluster of bunkers known as the Principal's Nose and at the wire fence defining out of bounds along the right. He knew the cautious player drove left of the bunkers to avoid a wild shot out of bounds, but this was not Palmer's way. Rejecting the careful line, he played a beautiful drive between the bunkers and the fence while Peter Baker and Baker-Finch took the safer route. Then, on the 17th, he played another daring drive aimed at the corner of the hotel to the right of the sheds. For a heart-stopping moment his ball looked as if it might hit the hotel wall, but it curled neatly away and settled in mid-fairway.

Still, Arnold bogeyed both. His driving reminded all of us of the young Palmer, but he couldn't take advantage of it. With a final wave to the adoring gallery, and to the clutch of players who waited by the green to watch his final strokes, Palmer walked off.

SECOND ROUND RESULTS

HOLE	1	2	3	4	5	6	7	8	9	10	11	12	13	14	15	16	17	18	
PAR	4	4	4	4	5	4	4	3	4	4	3	4	4	5	4	4	4	4	TOTAL
Brad Faxon	4	4	3	4	4	4	4	3	4	3	4	3	4	4	4	4	4	3	67-138
Katsuyoshi Tomori	4	4	4	4	4	4	3	3	4	4	3	3	5	4	4	3	4	4	68-138
John Daly	4	4	4	4	7	4	4	3	4	3	2	3	5	4	4	4	4	4	71-138
Ben Crenshaw	4	4	3	5	5	4	4	3	4	5	4	3	4	4	4	5	4	3	72-139
Marks Brooks	3	4	4	4	4	5	4	3	3	5	2	4	4	4	4	5	4	3	69-139
Costantino Rocca	4	3	4	4	4	4	3	3	4	4	3	5	4	5	4	4	5	3	70-139
John Cook	3	3	4	4	5	4	4	4	3	5	3	3	4	5	4	4	4	4	70-139
Ernie Els	4	3	3	4	5	4	4	3	4	3	3	3	3	4	5	4	5	4	68-139
Corey Pavin	4	4	3	4	5	4	4	3	4	3	3	4	4	5	4	5	4	3	70-139
Payne Stewart	3	4	4	5	4	4	4	4	4	3	4	3	4	4	3	4	4	3	68-140
Justin Leonard	3	4	4	4	4	4	4	3	4	4	3	3	4	3	4	4	4	4	67-140
Vijay Singh	4	4	4	5	5	4	3	4	4	4	4	3	4	4	4	4	5	3	72-140

HOLE SUMMARY

HOLE	PAR	EAGLES	BIRDIES	PARS	BOGEYS	HIGHER	RANK	AVERAGE
1	4	0	19	114	19	6	10	4.08
2	4	0	16	97	35	10	6	4.25
3	4	0	34	106	16	2	15	3.91
4	4	0	3	101	51	3	4	4.34
5	5	1	32	103	16	6	13	4.97
6	4	0	11	113	31	3	8	4.17
7	4	0	18	104	32	4	9	4.14
8	3	0	2	101	52	3	3	3.35
9	4	0	37	99	19	3	14	3.92
OUT	36	1	172	938	271	40		37.13
10	4	0	23	116	17	2	12	3.99
11	3	0	5	67	74	12	1	3.61
12	4	3	55	82	15	3	16	3.75
13	4	0	13	98	39	8	5	4.28
14	5	4	69	74	8	3	17	4.60
15	4	0	21	115	19	3	11	4.04
16	4	0	16	103	33	6	7	4.20
17	4	0	4	75	60	19	2	4.62
18	4	0	65	78	13	1	17	3.68
IN	36	7	271	808	278	57		36.77
TOTAL	72	8	443	1746	549	97		73.90

Players Below Par	35			
Players At Par	20			
Players Above Par	102			

LOW SCORES		
Low First Nine	*Steven Webster	32
Low Second Nine	Paul Lawrie	32
	Payne Stewart	32
Low Round	Nick Faldo	67
	Brad Faxon	67
	Justin Leonard	67

Approximately 180,000 spectators, including 40,000 on Friday, attended the 124th Open Championship.

Arnold Palmer said farewell to the Open Championship after 35 years.

PALMER'S FINAL HURRAH

BY BEV NORWOOD

The road alongside the 18th fairway was overflowing with spectators, and people filled the balconies and open windows of the adjoining buildings as Arnold Palmer, at the age of 65, played the last tee shot of his final Open Championship. Those in the grandstand behind the 17th green were standing and applauding after Palmer hit and began walking towards the ancient stone Swilcan Bridge just ahead. He paused as he reached the bridge, turned and removed his visor to wave towards them. The tribute continued down the fairway while Palmer completed his round with a two-putt par for 75 and a 158 total, which would be 10 strokes above the cut for 36 holes. His score hardly mattered to anyone other than Palmer himself.

Among those behind the green were other contestants, spanning the spectrum of professional golf. There was Palmer's contemporary, Lee Trevino, who had left the first tee before he was about to play. This would also be Trevino's final Open, but he had kept silent about that, out of respect for Palmer. The current stars included Nick Faldo, who had waited back after finishing his round. There as well was Tom Wargo, who had Palmer to thank for a mid-life career known as the Senior PGA Tour, and David Duval, a promising newcomer to the game.

All were there to salute the man who 35 years ago had restored the sagging fortunes of the Open Championship by his presence at St Andrews.

They had given Palmer the send-off everyone had anticipated in 1990 at St Andrews but did not happen then because when Palmer finished his second round at level par, he appeared safely under the cut. In a perfectly calm afternoon, the scores tumbled and Palmer was gone without fanfare. 'I did say then that I was not returning,' he said, 'but then a lot of people, mostly the Press, started saying, "Why don't you come back and play at St Andrews? You ought to finish on a better note than last time."' He thought he had an exemption for one more year and did not realize until after the fact that the Championship Committee had to make a minor amendment (to include past champions '65 or under') for him.

This was not like one year ago when Palmer played in his final US Open at Oakmont, in his home region of western Pennsylvania. He had been choked with emotion then, and was trying not to be again, although easily he could have, if he dared dwell on the sentiments of the thousands around him or, just afterwards, of those waiting for him in the interview tent. 'I guess it's over,' Palmer said, when he first sat before the Press, uncharacteristically seeming to avoid eye contact for the moment, and sipping a small whisky for the occasion. When asked about his thoughts during the round, he said, 'I was thinking of things that had nothing to do with my golf, and you cannot do that ... Today I promised myself that I was not going to get sentimental, so don't ask me too many questions I cannot answer.'

Nevertheless, Palmer enthusiastically shared the memories with his questioners. 'I cannot help but remember all those years that I have had and enjoyed, and that is most important,' he began. 'When I came up the 18th, I kept thinking about 1960 and what that led to ... a lot of great years and a lot of happy times for me, both in golf and socially. I thought about losing to Kel Nagle here and then winning at Birkdale (in 1961) and Troon (in 1962) and the things that happened subsequently, the friendships and the golf that we played. It has been a very happy situation, and I was reminded of that today.

'Going up the 18th I was looking at all the people and all the buildings, and it was a warming and happy time for me.'

Palmer recalled having to play two pre-qualifying rounds in 1960, and again in 1961 and 1962, as everyone did in those years, 'and the young players

Palmer said, 'This week I thought I would play better than I did.'

here this week did not believe it. They thought that Arnold Palmer never had to qualify for anything ... The younger players do not believe these things happened in those days. There are a lot of things like that that are now pleasant memories.'

On the Tuesday evening, Palmer had attended the Past Champions Dinner, which is traditional before Opens at St Andrews. 'I reflected in my remarks about the Open Championship what it has meant to me and to golf,' he said. 'The significance of the Open is that it is the tournament that is most watched and most revered in the entire world. I said in my remarks that we have a responsibility to the people who come into golf to protect the tradition and the quality of the game, and I feel very strongly about that.'

It was far different in 1995 than when Palmer came to St Andrews in 1960 for the Centenary of the world's oldest golf competition. American interest in the Open Championship had dwindled, and so had the stature of the event, since the majority of the best professionals then were Americans. The downslide began after 1930, when an American amateur, Bobby Jones, who was loved by the townspeople of St Andrews as if he were one of their own, completed the Grand Slam by winning the Open and Amateur titles of both Britain and the United States.

After the Second World War, no more than a handful of Americans were ever to be seen at any

Open venue. It remained that way until Palmer came along. He was the most popular player the game had known, and if the Open was important to Palmer, it was important to everyone. This year, American qualifiers even out-numbered residents of the United Kingdom, which perhaps was a first, if such records were kept, by 55 to 52.

There is no doubt this has been due to Palmer, who appropriately was influenced by Jones. As a result, Palmer not only restored the Open Championship to its rightful place in golf but also revived the concept of the Grand Slam. Palmer had been told about St Andrews and the game's Scottish origins by his father, Deacon, who had the dual role of golf professional and greenkeeper at Latrobe Country Club, but who had never been to Britain. When Palmer won the US Amateur in 1954, he had wanted to duplicate Jones' feat but could not afford to remain an amateur, as he eagerly recalled early in the week.

Palmer had the responsibilities of a newly-wed husband and, despite having become a professional in 1955, it was not until five years later that he first came to Britain or played in the Open Championship. He won his second Masters in April of that year, then the US Open in June. Flying from Denver to New York for the trip to Scotland, Palmer shared his ambition with the golf reporter from the *Pittsburgh Press*, Palmer's home newspaper, Bob Drum, who also returned for this year's Open.

'I said I would have the chance to leave Scotland with the chance for the modern Grand Slam,' Palmer recalled. 'He said, "What are you talking about?" I said I wanted to play and do what Jones did, and I could not afford it, and now I have the opportunity as a professional to do just the same thing ... I said if I can win here and go to the PGA with a little more confidence, I can have a shot at winning that.'

Before Palmer, no one had promoted those four tournaments in that context, but Drum wrote about it, and when Palmer arrived in St Andrews, he discussed it with Pat Ward-Thomas, Leonard Crawley and other British journalists. They too thought it was a splendid idea, this modern Grand Slam. It was not to be for Palmer in 1960 at St Andrews.

The last two rounds in those years were played on the Friday. 'I remember it like it was yesterday,' Palmer said, 'being at Rusacks and looking out the window after I had finished my morning round. There were some thunderstorms around, and Winnie said, 'If it keeps this up, you won't play this afternoon.' I said in the history of the Open it has never been cancelled for anything. It has always finished. She said it doesn't look very good. It rained like you can't believe ... They cancelled the final round on that day and they played on Saturday, which they had not done in past history.

'It disappointed me a lot ... I felt if I could have played again that afternoon, I would have won the Open then.'

Along with the Palmers for the trip were his father and a family friend, Harry Saxman. 'My father had one of the greatest weeks of his life here, and the week confirmed what I had thought all along,' he said. Unlike Sam Snead after his victory in 1946 or Ben Hogan after his in 1953, Palmer kept coming back. This year was his 23rd Open. 'I enjoyed it, so I came back,' he said. 'It was as simple as that. I enjoyed coming, I enjoyed the people, I made a lot of friends and enjoyed coming back.'

Remarkably, considering what happened after his first Open, those friends included several journalists. They talked Palmer and Gary Player into staying on and playing in the French Open. 'I said I had not entered,' Palmer recalled. 'They said don't worry

Palmer finished in style, holing this putt.

about that, we will enter you. I said okay, I will play. They said the same thing to Gary.' The Palmers spent the next week with a friend at Sculthorpe, Major George Vogel. He practised and played exhibitions for the US Air Force, then they were flown to Paris on a military C-47 (or DC-3) with steel seats in a thunderstorm. When they arrived for the French Open, Palmer said, 'We were rejected. We were told to go home. And we did just that. I never let Pat Ward-Thomas forget it.'

In an interview before this year's Open, Palmer was asked about his target for the week. 'There is only one,' he said, and everyone knew he meant victory. 'Because I am 65 that doesn't stop me from having the same target. It is still my target.' Would Palmer ever play in the Open again? 'I may come back in 2000, but it would only be to watch.' Not next year? 'Only to defend.' Back with the Press after his second round, Palmer said, 'This week I thought I would play better than I did. The first two holes yesterday destroyed me. When I four-putted from the fringe at the second, it burst my bubble.'

For his final day at the Open, Palmer wore a blue cashmere sweater that bore the emblem of the Royal and Ancient Golf Club of St Andrews. He said he was planning to return in September to play in the R and A's Autumn Meeting. He said jokingly, 'Since I played like one (a member) this week, I may as well act like one.'

Palmer said, 'Going up the 18th I was looking at all the people and all the buildings, and it was a warming and happy time.'

Costantino Rocca (209) drove the 12th green and made an eagle putt from 15 feet.

DAY

3

A GREAT, GREAT, GREAT DAY

BY ROBERT SOMMERS

At dusk on Saturday evening, hours after the last putt of the Open's third round had fallen, it had become obvious that none of the old heroes would claim the championship the following afternoon. Nick Price, the 1994 champion, had fallen to 16th place even though he shot 70, Nick Faldo to 29th by shooting a frustrating 75, and Greg Norman to 40th place after a 72. They had too many strokes to make up and too few holes left to do it. Norman stood 10 strokes out of first place, Faldo nine, and Price seven. In other times any one of them might have shot a round of 62 — they had done it often enough in the past — but not one of them had shown the confidence or the fire to recover those lost strokes. So far only Faldo had managed a round in the 60s, but then he went from 67, his best round, to 75, his worst. The 1995 Open Championship would be left to other men.

The leading contender at the moment was Michael Campbell, a 26-year-old Maori descended from a Scotsman who emigrated to New Zealand in the middle of the 19th century. Campbell startled the field by playing the Old Course in 65 on a windy, gusty day that had dried out the ground and turned some greens to the consistency of concrete. Somehow Campbell managed them, then climaxed his round with an improbable shot from the Road Bunker that rolled within 18 inches of the hole and saved his par 4.

His 65 led to a 54-hole score of 207, nine strokes under par, two ahead of Costantino Rocca, who persisted in holding on, and three ahead of Steve Elkington, Corey Pavin, Ernie Els, Katsuyoshi Tomori and John Daly, who showed signs of cracking toward the end of the round. Campbell's 65 beat the next best score by three strokes. Barry Lane, Mark James and Per-Ulrik Johansson shot 68s, but at 213, Lane lagged six strokes behind Campbell, and James and Johansson trailed by eight. The probability they

could catch up seemed slight.

Meantime, Brad Faxon dropped six strokes behind with a spiritless 75 and began his gradual slide out of the race; Frank Nobilo, who had played two steady rounds of 70 and 71, fell apart in the rising wind and shot 80; and John Cook, just one stroke behind when the round began, shot 75 and dropped into a tie with Price in 16th place, headed backward.

At the same time, Sam Torrance, the always popular Scot, shot another 71 and held on at 212, five strokes back, tied with the American Mark Brooks, who slipped back with a round of 73. Brooks would be heard from later.

Once again the wind played a serious role in the scoring, rising from the southwest once more but now at velocities of up to 30 miles an hour, the strongest yet. It tore in dead into the face of those playing the first hole, and it shortened the 18th considerably. The outward nine, then, figured to play harder than the holes leading home. Jack Nicklaus, for example, laboured over the first nine. Among the early starters, he played the outward nine in 40 after taking seven strokes on the fifth, but with the wind at his back he came home in 37. It had not been a good week.

Campbell had attracted only passing interest through the early rounds, even though he had shot two respectable 71s. He had gone into the third round in a tie for 20th place and had teed off at 12.54, over two hours before Faxon and Tomori, the last men to start. By the time they struck their first shots, Campbell had already birdied four holes and had turned for home in 32. Six under par now, he had caught the leaders.

Even though he had to fight the strong wind crossing from left to right that forced shots toward the thick stands of gorse bordering the right of the outward holes, Campbell played some outstanding irons and putted like a dream. He might have lost a shot at

Michael Campbell (207) had a near-perfect shot at the 17th, his ball catching the slope of the bunker.

Steve Elkington (210) missed this 10-foot putt at the 17th.

the second after leaving his seven-iron approach short, but he chipped within six feet and holed the putt.

Buoyed by the save, he nearly eagled the third with a pitch that settled barely three inches from the cup, and then he ran in a putt from 30 feet on the fifth, his second birdie. First-rate irons left him within 10 feet on each of the next three, and he birdied both the seventh and ninth for his 32.

When Campbell's score went up on the leaderboard, others found it hard to believe. Playing three holes behind him, Torrance recalled, 'I couldn't keep my eyes off the scoreboard. Every time I looked his score kept getting better.'

Playing in the easier wind coming back, Campbell missed another 10-footer on the 11th, the devilish par 3 where the pin was set a little more than 15 feet behind the Strath Bunker, but then he began a run of three straight birdies. He drove the 12th green and got down in two from 40 feet, lofted a sand wedge to 10 feet on the 13th and holed it, overshot the 14th, the par 5, with a four-iron second but chipped back and holed from 10 feet once again.

Now he stood seven under par for the day, nine under for 50 holes. Finally leading the field now, he saw no one making a run at him. Faxon had double-bogeyed the sixth and gone out in 39, Tomori was on his way to 37, Daly and Crenshaw were both stumbling, and although Rocca continued to play nice, steady golf, he stood four strokes behind Campbell and needed something better.

Campbell nearly gave it to him on the 17th, where his nine-iron approach missed the narrow green and splashed into the Road Bunker. He still felt confident enough, but when he walked up to his ball, he found it settled into a nearly impossible position, hardly more than a foot from the high, revetted front wall. Now he faced a serious situation. His ball lay in such a confining space he couldn't play to the left, he couldn't play it to the right, and he didn't have the room to play it backwards and away from the green. It seemed unlikely he could play any kind of shot that would clear the bunker's face; if he tried, it seemed likely he would waste a shot and still leave his ball in the sand.

Briefly he considered declaring his ball unplayable and dropping within the bunker but farther from the front bank, but his ball might bury. With no other apparent option, and with the confidence of youth, he decided to play it. He had in fact experimented with this shot in practice rounds early in the week and felt sure he could dig the ball out, but he only hoped to finish 20 feet or so left of the hole.

Meantime, seeing the lie on television back in the R and A clubhouse, Gary Player, one of the game's finest bunker players ever, checked with R and A members to be sure Campbell could indeed invoke the unplayable ball rule and drop away from the bank. Assured that the rule could be applied, Player said, 'Then that's what he should do.'

Naturally, Campbell didn't. He dug in his feet, aimed left of the flagstick, set just 15 feet from the bunker, then swung into the shot. The ball shot up quickly, but as it climbed toward the top of the bank, it grazed against the layered sod. Campbell sucked in his breath, afraid the ball would drop back into the sand and perhaps even hit him, which would cost him two penalty strokes in addition to the wasted shot.

Instead, the ball hit the edge of the bunker's face, took the slope of the ground, then slowly trickled toward the cup. It rolled within a foot or so of the hole. The gallery seated in the huge grandstand across

Corey Pavin (211) had 'a lot of long putts' in his 72.

John Daly (211) made 3 on the 18th after 6 on the 17th.

the road broke into a thundering roar, and Campbell took a deep breath.

Seeing the result of the shot, Player rose from his chair, clapped a few times, then bowed toward the television set. It had indeed been a miraculous shot. Campbell said, 'So easily I could have lost three or four shots.' Instead, he had come back in 33 and shot the best round of the championship, a score no one would match.

While his position at the top of the standings may have surprised most of the gallery, others more familiar with European golf felt it might have been inevitable since Campbell was in his first year on the PGA European Tour and making a success of it. He had placed second to Bernhard Langer in the Volvo PGA Championship eight weeks earlier and had fin-

ished among the leading 10 scorers in four other European tournaments. A year ago he had missed the cut by two strokes at Turnberry in his first Open.

A powerfully built 5-foot-10, with brown skin, dark hair and coal black eyes, Campbell can trace one ancestor to Scotland. Logan Campbell had emigrated from Edinburgh in 1845 and settled in Auckland, the northernmost of New Zealand's major cities. He eventually became Auckland's mayor. The name Campbell survived through the generations, but there seems to be little Scottish blood left, for Campbell is a Maori, the Polynesian people who settled in New Zealand before Captain Cook claimed the islands for Britain.

Meantime, while Campbell accepted congratulations, others struggled through the difficult conditions. As Campbell holed his birdie putt on the 13th, Daly and Crenshaw watched from the adjoining fifth green. Crenshaw had bogeyed two holes by then, and Daly had opened with a bogey 5 on the first, and so they had fallen behind Campbell by then. Crenshaw birdied the fifth, going back to four under par, but whatever hopes he might have had were lost on the ninth and 10th, strangely enough because of his putting.

Crenshaw drove nicely on the ninth to a nice position behind End Hole Bunker, a drive of about 300 yards that left him a little pitch to the hole, cut in the left rear about 20 feet from the green's edge. With the wind slightly behind him, he nipped the ball crisply enough to make it brake on that hard green and pull up no more than 15 or 18 feet from the cup.

With the wind growing stronger by the minute, Ben rolled his first putt perhaps three feet past, then missed. Instead of a birdie, he bogeyed and played the first nine in 39. He hit another good drive on the 10th, but a loose pitch left him too far from the hole to think of a birdie, and once again he three-putted. These were two holes where he must have expected to pick up one stroke, and instead he lost two. Birdies on the 15th and 16th helped some, but then his pitch to the 17th ran into the Road Bunker, he took two strokes to recover, double-bogeyed, and finished the round with 76. He played no further part in the championship.

Ernie Els (211) was not happy with his chip to the 17th green, but still got his par.

Katsuyoshi Tomori (211) bogeyed the 16th and 17th holes, finishing with 73.

Sam Torrance (212) had 'a real chance of winning.'

Brett Ogle (213) made a birdie on the 18th.

Daly, meanwhile, had driven the ninth, birdied there, then drove the 12th and birdied again. Six under par once again, he stood three strokes behind Campbell. It didn't last. He bogeyed the 15th, made his par on the 16th, then moved on to the 17th, the most dangerous hole in championship golf.

As he had done in the second round, Daly missed the fairway. He had driven with his one iron, but instead of drifting right, as it must do to catch the fairway, the ball turned left. Daly knew right away he had hit a bad shot; he released the club with his right hand as soon as he made contact.

Daly can be impatient at times. Here he chopped the ball from the rough into the Scholars Bunker along the left, short of the green, then quickly flailed at it again, pitching it back to the fairway. Like Crenshaw, he made 6. Just four under par now, five behind Campbell, Daly planned to fade his drive on the 18th, but his foot slipped as he moved into the downswing and the ball shot off straight. For a moment John was afraid it might run over the green and out of bounds, but it hit the concrete steps leading from the first tee toward the members' car park and rebounded back into play. Daly rolled his ball within eight feet of the cup and birdied. Back in par 36, he shot 73, dropping from a tie for first into a tie for fourth place, behind not only Campbell but Rocca and Elkington as well.

A chunky, agreeable Italian, Rocca went off with Brooks in the third from last group. A 34-year-old Texan who, like Ben Hogan, has spent his life in Fort Worth, Brooks had won four tournaments in his 11

Tom Watson (213) birdied the 10th.

Barry Lane (213) went round in 68 and climbed to a share of 10th place, six strokes behind the leader.

years on the American PGA Tour, but only one since 1991. He had been a contender in the 1990 US Open, but had finished with 73 and missed tying Hale Irwin and Mike Donald by three strokes. He had begun the Open with two steady rounds of 70 and 69, but he played loose golf through most of the third round and stood four over par through the 13th. Then he rallied by birdieing the 14th and closed with a rush with birdie 3s on both the 17th and 18th. His 73 kept him close enough to make a serious run at the championship the next day.

Rocca could indeed have caught Campbell with a stronger finish. Out in 36, he had played through the hardest part of the course without surrendering strokes, then drove the 12th and holed from 15 feet for an eagle 2. He had begun the day at five under par and now he stood at seven under, just two behind.

With the help of the following wind, a drive and a five iron put him on the 14th green just 20 feet from the hole. His first putt missed, but he holed the second. Eight under now for the 50 holes he had played, he was one stroke behind. Safely on the 16th green with two iron shots, Rocca faced a 15-foot putt that could tie him for the lead, but he went a little too boldly for the cup. His first putt slipped about three feet past and he missed coming back. Instead of catching Campbell, Rocca had dropped two strokes behind him.

He had two more chances but missed them both from 10 feet and shot 70, two under par for the day, seven under for the distance.

Bob Estes (213) shot 71 with a 4, 3 finish.

Among the Americans who had less prominent roles than expected were, clockwise from top left, Lee Janzen (217), amateur Tiger Woods (217), Peter Jacobsen (217) and Davis Love III (222).

Brad Faxon (213) went out in 39, with 6 on the fourth.

Mark James (215) had 32 on the inward nine.

By then Elkington had finished with his second consecutive 69 after opening with 72, and he certainly looked as if he had the measure of the Old Course. He had gone out in 35 with easy birdies on the first and third — the first from just one foot and the third from six feet — and a bogey on the ninth. Again he hit an approach stiff to the flagstick and birdied the 13th from four feet, then reached the 14th green with his second but had to struggle for the birdie, saving it from 10 feet. Three under for the day, he could make up no more ground and finished the second nine in 34. At 210 he stood three strokes behind Campbell, in position to make up ground if Michael foundered.

Campbell had no doubt he wouldn't because he had set his goals so high. Earlier in the year he said he had ambitions to become the best player in the world.

'People told me I shouldn't say that, but I believe I have the ability, the attitude, and all the right stuff to be the best in the world,' he said. 'When you can go out and compete against the best players in the game, you grow in confidence and start to believe you can win the big one.'

Once again he spoke of his Scottish ancestor, Logan Campbell.

'He was my great, great, great-grandfather, and this was a great, great, great day.'

Vijay Singh (213) shot 73 in the third round.

THIRD ROUND RESULTS

HOLE	1	2	3	4	5	6	7	8	9	10	11	12	13	14	15	16	17	18	
PAR	4	4	4	4	5	4	4	3	4	4	3	4	4	5	4	4	4	4	TOTAL
Michael Campbell	4	4	3	4	4	4	3	3	3	4	3	3	3	4	4	4	4	4	65-207
Costantino Rocca	4	3	4	4	5	4	4	4	4	4	3	2	4	4	4	5	4	4	70-209
Steve Elkington	3	4	3	4	5	4	4	3	5	4	3	4	3	4	4	4	5	3	69-210
Corey Pavin	3	5	4	4	5	4	4	4	4	4	3	4	4	4	5	4	3		72-211
Ernie Els	5	4	4	4	5	4	4	3	5	4	3	4	5	4	4	3	4	3	72-211
John Daly	5	4	4	4	5	4	4	4	3	4	3	3	4	4	5	4	6	3	73-211
Katsuyoshi Tomori	4	4	4	5	5	4	5	3	3	4	3	3	4	4	4	5	5	4	73-211
Sam Torrance	4	5	4	4	4	5	4	3	4	4	3	4	4	4	4	4	4	3	71-212
Mark Brooks	4	5	4	4	5	5	4	3	5	4	4	4	4	4	4	4	3	3	73-212
Barry Lane	5	4	4	4	4	4	4	3	4	3	3	3	3	4	4	3	5	4	68-213
Tom Watson	4	3	4	4	5	4	4	3	4	3	5	3	4	5	4	3	4	4	70-213
Brett Ogle	5	5	4	5	4	4	4	3	3	3	3	3	5	4	3	5	5	3	71-213
Bob Estes	4	4	4	4	5	5	4	3	4	3	3	4	4	4	5	4	3	71-213
Vijay Singh	4	5	3	5	5	4	4	4	3	5	3	4	4	4	5	4	4	73-213
Brad Faxon	5	4	4	6	5	4	4	2	5	4	4	3	5	4	4	4	4	4	75-213

HOLE SUMMARY

HOLE	PAR	EAGLES	BIRDIES	PARS	BOGEYS	HIGHER	RANK	AVERAGE
1	4	1	11	63	27	1	9	4.16
2	4	0	5	66	27	5	4	4.31
3	4	0	17	72	13	1	14	3.98
4	4	0	1	51	44	7	2	4.55
5	5	0	10	70	17	6	10	5.18
6	4	0	8	73	19	3	8	4.17
7	4	0	10	80	12	1	13	4.04
8	3	0	7	68	28	0	6	3.20
9	4	2	25	55	19	2	15	3.94
OUT	36	3	94	598	206	26		37.53
10	4	0	11	72	17	3	11	4.12
11	3	0	10	66	22	5	3	3.24
12	4	2	42	49	9	1	16	3.66
13	4	0	8	63	28	4	5	4.28
14	5	7	54	34	6	2	18	4.47
15	4	0	10	79	13	1	12	4.05
16	4	0	8	63	32	0	7	4.23
17	4	0	4	40	51	8	1	4.63
18	4	0	43	59	1	0	17	3.59
IN	36	9	190	525	179	24		36.27
TOTAL	72	12	284	1123	385	50		73.80

			LOW SCORES		
Players Below Par	24				
Players At Par	15		Low First Nine	Michael Campbell	32
Players Above Par	64			Hisayuki Sasaki	32
			Low Second Nine	Mark James	32
				Barry Lane	32
			Low Round	Michael Campbell	65

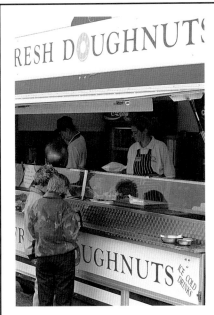

The Open Championship offered a wide variety of sights, refreshments and activities.

Michael Campbell, 150 years after his forefather emigrated to New Zealand, became a Scottish favourite.

CAMPBELL MAKES AN IMPACT

BY ALISTER NICOL

Michael Campbell did not so much swim into the ken of millions of world-wide television watchers with his third-round 65 over the Old Course, he burst from relative obscurity to instant recognition like some predator of the deep crashing to the surface of the ocean. The self-assured young New Zealander's impact was immediate, and the ripples of his seven-under-par 65, which settled him atop the leaderboards on that Saturday night, may soon reach the shores of every land where golf is played.

The Maori, whose great, great, great-grandfather left his native Edinburgh in 1845 and settled in New Zealand the following year and went on to take a native woman as one of his wives, can play. He had proved his ability around the world long before he arrived in St Andrews for the 124th Open to set the championship alight with one of the greatest, to say nothing of most fortuitous, sand saves from the notorious Road Bunker en route to his bogey-free 65.

In 1992, Campbell crossed the Pacific to Canada and led New Zealand's amateur side to victory in the prestigious Eisenhower Trophy at Capilano Golf Club in British Columbia. That same year he took the Australian Amateur title, and those twin feats earned him the New Zealand Young Sportsman of the Year and Australian Amateur Golfer of the Year awards.

It was then a short and inevitable step to professionalism, and one which Campbell comfortably took in his stride in 1993. He had three top-10 finishes in his first four starts and his first victory, in Australia's Canon Challenge, was by a three-stroke margin. He added the title of Rookie of the Year in Australasia to his growing, and glowing, honours board after finishing seventh on the Order of Merit.

By now, Michael had determined that golf in the Antipodes was too restricting for his burgeoning talents so, in time-honoured fashion, he took himself off to Europe. Like countless Southern Hemisphere golfers before him, including defending champion Nick Price and past champion Greg Norman, Campbell chose to enrol in golf's toughest finishing school.

If the PGA European Tour is tough, the satellite circuit, known as the Challenge Tour, is even more rigourous. That is where, in 1994, Campbell had to prove himself good enough to join the big boys such as European No. 1 Colin Montgomerie and Sam Torrance from the land of his forefather. He was more than up to the Challenge. In a burst of midsummer form, he thrust aside his failures to qualify for the US Open at Oakmont and, in three successive appearances, won three tournaments.

The first was the St Louis Open on the Tommy Armour Tour, which he entered for the simple reason that he was in the United States anyway. Buoyed by that US$40,000 worth of success, he recrossed the Atlantic to win the Memorial Olivier Barras event in Switzerland before crossing the Alps to win the Bank of Austria Open. In total Campbell competed in seven Challenge Tour events in Europe, recorded two wins and three other top-10 finishes to wind up third in the Order of Merit and gain automatic membership on the PGA European Tour.

His growing maturity did not go unnoticed Down Under, and when Australasia played Southern Africa in the inaugural Alfred Dunhill Challenge early in 1995, Campbell was in captain Terry Gales' Australasian team. He partnered Norman in a four-ball match against David Frost and Retief Goosen in mile-high Johannesburg and proved he had more than a head for heights.

Frost was in devastating form that beautiful day with 10 birdies in 15 holes as he and his partner swept to a convincing 3-and-1 victory. One might have expected the battle-hardened Norman to do most of the work in trying to stem such a tidal wave of sub-par scoring, but in fact it was his young

Campbell learned the Old Course from several veterans.

partner who battled hardest. Only the fact that Campbell was eight under par on his own ball kept the margin reasonably respectable, with Norman little more than an unhappy spectator.

By the time Campbell reached the Home of Golf for the Open Championship, he had already compiled a highly impressive record on the 1995 PGA European Tour. In 13 starts he had missed only three cuts and carded five top-10 finishes, the best being tied for second behind Bernhard Langer in the Volvo PGA Championship at Wentworth. His bank balance had been increased by £186,220 as a result of his classy play, and the cognoscenti were well aware he was one of the men to watch at St Andrews.

His third-round play came as no surprise to Price and Australian Steve Elkington. Recalled Price, 'I first played with Michael in the 1992 New Zealand Open when he was still an amateur and I was very impressed. He is a very good young player.' Said Elkington, 'I am one of the few players not surprised by his play. I played with him in the Australian Masters a few years ago, and I have been telling everyone since he is going to be a sensational player. He has a great swing which I think will hold up for him, and playing on the European Tour will help him mature. He has a terrific future.'

Price, Norman, former-champion Ian Baker-Finch, Craig Parry and US veteran Raymond Floyd partnered Campbell in practice over the Old Course, offering him priceless advice and encouragement. 'They told me everything about the course,' he acknowledged. 'They said to watch out for this pot bunker, play it left here, be short of the flag on this hole, past the flag on another hole. They pointed out everything from where to hit my drives and second shots to how to handle the greens.

'Greg Norman, particularly, has been a great help since I turned professional.'

Those tips from the top were quickly assimilated by the youngster, who is alert and aware enough to know that by serving an apprenticeship, so to speak, on the European Tour he would learn how to play a variety of shots and handle the wind before moving on to lusher pastures. He has learned well.

Just how well he proved on the third day when the wind, though warm and a good few knots short of a gale, proved more than a little troublesome for most. Not Campbell, however. He was out in 32 with birdies at all the odd-numbered holes apart from the first, where he carefully two-putted for par, having hit a six-iron approach over the Burn to a safe 30 feet. He then cut loose with three successive birdies from the 12th to stretch away from the field. His drive at the 12th made the green and he two-putted for his 3. He knocked in a 10-footer at the 13th for another 3, and at the long 14th drained a 10-footer for his birdie 4 to go seven under for his round.

His approach to the fiendishly difficult 17th green found the Road Bunker. Even worse, it was mere inches from the revetted face of the bunker, which is as sheer and, to the golfer standing there, as high as the North Face of the Eiger. All the portents were that his previous good work would be largely negated by the bunker.

Campbell had an horrific lie. He could not play out to the right, to the left or even backwards and, though he briefly contemplated taking a penalty drop, was afraid to do so lest the ball bury in an even more difficult lie. So he played it as it lay, and it is now part of Open lore that the ball, miraculously, ended barely 18 inches from the cup for a tap-in par.

He later confessed, 'All I was trying to do was get the ball within 20 feet or so of the flag. Craig Parry and I had practised the shot earlier in the week, and I knew I could get it out. But today the ball hit the face two or three feet from the top, popped up in the air and for a second I thought it was going to come back on me. But it just popped up there and rolled down towards the cup. Someone up there was smiling down on me at that moment. I could easily have dropped three or four shots at that hole. I was very fortunate to make 4.'

Following his great escape, he missed his birdie at the last from just 10 feet and said, 'The 18th is very birdieable and it would have been nice to have shot 64 instead of 65, but even 65 is unbelievable in only my second Open. I did everything right from tee to green and as well as playing great I putted great.

'I have watched the Open on television since I was 12, and I have said to myself that one day I would be there to play alongside the great players who are all my role models. That gave me the motivation to work hard, and here I am leading the Open after three rounds. It is a fantastic feeling.'

A closing 76 to share third place, one stroke behind, did not dampen Campbell's enthusiasm. 'I'm happy but disappointed,' he said. 'I had my chances, but it was not to be … I have learnt a lot. That walk up the last fairway was something special, and to receive a standing ovation … This is my second British Open, and to come third is a nice achievement.'

That great, great, great-grandfather of his who emigrated from Scotland 150 years ago made a huge success of his life. Knighted as Sir Logan Campbell, he became Mayor of Auckland and a very popular one at that, particularly among the Maori who adored the white man in their midst so much they dedicated the city's One Tree Hill to him. 'He is

A par on the 18th completed Campbell's special day.

pretty famous in New Zealand,' Michael said. 'I guess I am now too.'

Should great, great, great-grandson continue to improve and mature there is every likelihood that in the not-too-distant future he will become New Zealand's first Open champion since Bob Charles as long ago as 1963. Michael Campbell seems destined to go a long way in his career and he will never, ever forget that bunker shot at the 17th on the third round of the 124th Open Championship at St Andrews. Nor will anyone else who saw it.

John Daly (282), with a 30-foot birdie on the second hole, took a two-stroke lead in the play-off.

DALY PROVES HIS METTLE

BY ROBERT SOMMERS

Shortly after he finished his last round of the Open, hours before the leaders were to start, Jack Nicklaus announced that, one — this was possibly his last Open until 2000, and, two — he didn't think John Daly had much chance to win.

As later events showed, Nicklaus, the finest player of his time, is a poor prophet, for not only did Daly win, he won after having his heart ripped from him when Costantino Rocca holed the most improbable putt in living memory, a putt across the 18th green that rolled at least 60 feet through the Valley of Sin, climbed a gentle slope, and suddenly found the cup directly in its path. It dived in — if it hadn't it would have run yards past — and Rocca had forced a four-hole play-off.

The play-off was anti-climactic; Rocca was spent by then, and Daly won easily.

Like that astonishing putt, the entire last day of the 124th Open Championship had been filled with the tension of unexpected developments, first with Nicklaus' thoughts of giving up his annual visit to the championship he had graced every year since 1962; with the sudden blossoming of Steven Bottomley as a threat; the stumbling start of Michael Campbell, which cost him the championship; the gritty play of Rocca throughout the day, especially over the last few holes; and transcending them all, the realization that Daly is indeed a three-dimensional player — he can do much more than hammer the ball.

If the 1995 Open proved a point, it was that Daly is good enough to win anything at all. He had come into the championship as a mystery; the whole world knew he hit the ball out of sight, but then he astonished us all with his all-around ability, especially his delicate touch around and on the greens, and his surprising flair for playing the running shots so necessary for links golf. He had been known to sulk and play as if he didn't care when the ball didn't run his

way, but when he played a hole or two poorly at St Andrews, he gathered himself and struck back. His reaction when Rocca holed his unlikely putt on the 18th showed he had the will to win.

Neither that will, which Daly hadn't shown in the past, nor his method of playing his shots prompted much confidence in him, but then of the nine men within five strokes of one another when the day began, only Corey Pavin, fresh from winning the US Open, and Ernie Els, who had won it a year earlier, would have drawn more support, other than Campbell, who was the leader at nine under par, and Rocca, who was in second place at seven under.

When the wind came up early in the day, Daly's method seemed to be against him.

Once again the wind came in out of the west but stronger, occasionally gusting to 45 miles an hour, strong enough to turn the final round into an exacting test of the game without making it impossible, although others felt differently. Turning in a second successive 75, Nick Faldo said, 'It's the worst wind I can remember in an Open. Balls on the green were likely to move, and trying to judge the wind when you were putting was so difficult.'

Nicklaus felt it would hurt Daly because he hits his shots high, and in a moment of recklessness he added he didn't believe John had much chance. 'Look for Tom Watson,' he said. 'He's the best bad-weather player out there.' Another bad prediction; Watson shot 77 and tied for 31st place.

Four strokes behind Campbell when the day began, Daly and Els had run off three pars when the gallery sensed that this might become a tight and tense finish. Playing eight groups from the end, Bottomley had birdied the fourth and fifth, dropping him to four under par, and Brooks had birdied the second, falling to five under. They had many strokes to make up, but they, at least, were making birdies.

Daly then made a move on the fourth, at 463 yards

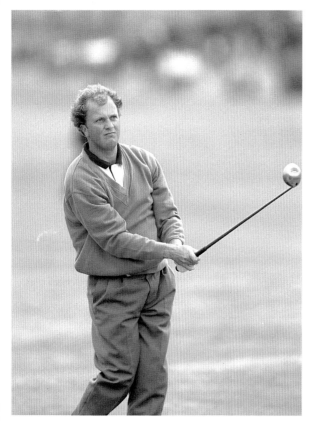

Steven Bottomley (283) made a surprising challenge.

Michael Campbell (283) saved par with this chip at the third, but more trouble lay ahead.

the longest par 4 on the course. A fine nine iron drifted with the wind, rolled 15 feet past the hole, and Daly holed it. He was six under par, now, just three behind Campbell, who was struggling.

Campbell had given nothing away, but he had holed a couple of four- and five-footers to save pars on the first two holes and had hit his approach so wide of the flagstick on the third he played his third shot with a pitching wedge even though his ball lay on the green. Once again he saved a par, but he was looking shaky indeed.

Play was becoming agonizingly slow. Every group waited between shots, sometimes as long as five minutes. Under these conditions the players had trouble keeping their rhythm from one shot to another, and it began to show. Pavin, usually a deadly putter, could hole nothing and gradually gave way. Els was playing loose golf. Katsuyoshi Tomori, the Japanese hope, was on his way to shooting 78; and Sam Torrance, five strokes behind when the day began, gave his followers hope when he birdied the third, but he gave away strokes on both the eighth and ninth when he needed more birdies.

The wind was causing nagging problems. Whipping trouser legs and bending flagsticks, it blew putts off line and indeed threatened to move balls on the greens. Some players cautiously avoided grounding their putters so they couldn't be penalized if the ball moved. Then a lashing rain fell from time to time. How much a role the conditions played in Campbell's first mistake can't be judged, but the wind howled across the fifth fairway from left to right as Campbell played his second shot.

From a good position in the fairway, about 220 yards out, Campbell ripped into his one iron. The shot was a disaster. Caught up in the wind, it soared off to the right, carried over the gorse bushes, passed behind the grandstand beside the green, and settled in a clean lie on the fourth fairway of the New Course, which runs parallel, more than 100 yards from the green. A nine iron into the wind pulled up 30 feet from the cup, and he three-putted, his first bogey since the 17th hole of the second round. He was eight under par now.

At about this time, Daly played a beautifully judged

Vijay Singh (284) had only two birdies. Steve Elkington (284) struggled. Sam Torrance (286) had hope early.

low, running shot into the seventh that pulled up within six feet of the cup. He holed it, and was seven under par and one stroke behind.

Now the entire complexion of the Open changed as Campbell and Rocca fell back and Daly surged ahead. An eight iron to 12 feet on the eighth followed by another good putt and Daly went to eight under just as Campbell drove into one of the Coffin Bunkers on the sixth. With no hope of reaching the green, he gave up another stroke, dropped to seven under, and fell behind Daly.

Meantime, Bottomley was having one of those days players of his calibre only dream of. Off more than an hour before the last pair, he had birdied both the fourth with a putt of about 14 feet, and the fifth by getting down in two from 100 feet. Then, after bogeying the eighth, he had one of those breaks that make all the difference between a good round and a bad one.

Short of the ninth green with his drive, Bottomley tried to play a running six-iron shot to the pin, cut in the back centre of the green, but he caught the shot fat and left his ball 75 feet short of the hole. Then he holed the putt. Out in 34, he had fallen to four under par, not contending yet, for Campbell hadn't begun his slide, but moving closer.

No matter what happened after this, though, Bottomley already had become the surprise of the Open. Not one of the bright lights of European golf, he had missed the cut in seven of his eight previous tournaments, had never placed higher than 10th since he joined the PGA European Tour in 1988, had gone through the qualifying tournament seven times, had missed the cut at Muirfield in 1987, his only other Open, and had won a place at St Andrews by holing a nine-foot putt on the final hole of qualifying. Now here he was in position to win the Open.

Six holes later he ran in another giant putt from 65 feet on the 15th, and now he stood five under par, and his dreams looked even better, for Campbell had begun giving away strokes, and although Daly had begun his run, he still had lots of hard holes to play.

A shot into the Road Bunker cost Bottomley one stroke, but he closed with a birdie from about six feet on the home hole, shot 69, the only player within 20 strokes of the lead to break 70, and finished with 283, five under par. It was the best score in; let the others try to match it.

Mark Brooks was the first. Beginning the day at 212, four under par, he was still four under approaching the 14th after birdieing the second and bogeying the 11th. His had not been a smooth round so far; he had struggled to save pars on three holes, including the 10th, where he holed from about 25 feet, and three-putted the 11th from an estimated 100 feet when his tee shot ran away from him in the

Mark Brooks (283) three-putted for a bogey here at the 11th, then took double bogey from Deacon Sime Bunker at the 16th.

crossing wind. But he had birdied the second, and now, with help from the wind, he went for the 14th green with his second shot. He made it, holed his second putt from 10 feet for one birdie, then punched a seven iron into the 15th green and holed from 25 feet. Now he stood six under par, just two behind Daly, who was playing two holes behind him.

Like Daly, Brooks had shown a knack for links golf, perhaps because he had taken the time to prepare himself. Not among the exempt players, he flew over early and arrived the Tuesday of the week before the Open, played Royal County Down, in Northern Ireland, one of the world's great courses; crossed over to Scotland and played Prestwick, Royal Troon and Western Gailes on the west coast; then shot 65 in qualifying and set a course record at Ladybank, where Bottomley had squeaked through in a play-off. Now he had the Open within reach if he could pick up another stroke on the last three holes.

Playing gambling golf now, Brooks threw himself into his driver. The ball streaked straight toward the 16th green, missed the Principal's Nose Bunkers, but somehow it kicked into another bunker called Deacon Sime just beyond it. Brooks was ruined. He could do no more than pitch out sideways, his third missed the green, and he took three more from there. He scored a double-bogey 6.

A closing birdie helped, but who knows what might have happened if Brooks' drive on the 16th had missed the bunker. Still, he had matched Bottomley at 283, and he had some hope, because Daly suddenly began losing strokes.

John had nearly ruined his round with a wild drive on the ninth. Three under par after his birdie on the eighth, Daly pulled his drive toward the gorse lining the left. If it settled in those bushes it could be unplayable — if he could find it at all.

Once again fortune smiled. His ball lay on a shell-lined path threading through the gorse. He could play it. Reprieved, he pitched short of the green, rolled his next shot within holing distance, and saved his par 4. He was still eight under for 63 holes.

After pars on 10 and 11, Daly's drive pulled up short of the 12th green, but he putted up the slope to the upper level within six feet of the cup. Another birdie here and he could run away from the field. He missed; the ball caught the lip of the hole but stayed out.

Three holes later his putt from 30 feet on the 15th slammed into the back of the cup and jumped out. Another missed birdie. Still eight under par, and now three strokes clear of Steve Elkington and Campbell, because by now Brooks had made his 6 on the 16th.

Elkington deserved better than he was getting because he had probably played the best tee-to-green golf of any of Daly's challengers, but he couldn't hole a putt. Hole after hole his ball skimmed past the cup. When another putt glided past the cup on the

16th, he had missed from holing distance on four consecutive holes. He eventually lost his chance when he bogeyed the 17th.

Rocca, meantime, had steadied himself after a shaky beginning. Level par through the first six holes, he bogeyed the seventh, eighth and 10th — his par putt on the 10th caught the lip and spun back toward him — but he birdied the 14th and matched Elkington at five under par as Daly teed off on the 16th.

Daly nearly threw it away over the next two holes. His approach to the 16th nearly reached the green's upper level, but turned away and slipped back down the slope into a hollow at the front. From perhaps 70 feet he putted 15 feet past and missed coming back. He was back to seven under and had only a two-stroke cushion now.

Once again his drive skipped across the 17th fair-

Daly fought for pars on the inward nine, then took 5 at the 16th and again at the 17th, when he hit into the Road Bunker.

Costantino Rocca (282) could not believe he had stubbed his chip shot beside the 18th green ...

way into the rough, and his second bounced into a terrible lie close to the face of the Road Bunker. Laying the blade of his wedge nearly flat, Daly swung into the ball with nearly all of his strength. It popped up, cleared the high, steep face, and bounded on to the green about 30 feet from the cup. He took two putts and had bogeyed once again. He was six under par now and only one stroke ahead of Rocca, who somehow had become the only man who might catch him. When Daly missed from 25 feet at the 18th, Rocca's opening widened. He needed just one more birdie to catch up and two to win outright.

Rocca missed his chance on the 16th, and when he mis-played his approach to the 17th, Daly seemed safe. Rocca's ball skirted the front of the green, shot across the road, slammed into the stone wall, then rebounded back on to the road and sat in a small depression. Only a miracle shot would save him now.

It is difficult to explain the range of emotions of the next few minutes as Rocca failed, succeeded,

... then Rocca holed a most improbable putt from about 60 feet through the Valley of Sin to tie Daly and force a

When Rocca's putt went in, the spectators round the 18th hole erupted with cheers that might be heard through the town.

play-off. He fell to the ground, buried his face, pounded his fists, and lay there while the gallery continued cheering.

Minutes later, Rocca met Daly on the first tee.

failed and succeeded once more, while Daly stood by watching himself being handed the championship, then having it snatched away.

First, Rocca did indeed play that impossible shot. Because the ball sat in the depression, he couldn't use a pitching club; he had to play his putter. Then, when he struck the ball, it popped up as if he had hit a pitching club, carried over the road, caught a piece of turf that shot it forward, climbed the bank, jumped on to the green, and rolled within four feet of the cup. Rocca saved his par 4. He was still five under with the vulnerable 18th to play.

When his drive pulled up left of the green, leaving him a simple pitch across the Valley of Sin, Rocca tried a risky shot. He wanted to play a pitch with enough backspin to brake quickly once it cleared the valley. As tense as he had ever been, with thousands

Rocca took 7 at the 17th hole in the play-off, including three shots from the Road Bunker.

84

Daly went two ahead on the first two play-off holes, then marched down the 18th fairway with a five-stroke lead.

watching from the grandstands and along The Links, Rocca stubbed the shot. His ball carried hardly more than 15 yards and rolled to the bottom of the valley, about 60 or so feet from the hole.

The sympathetic gallery groaned and Rocca hung his head while Daly's wife threw her arms around John, certain he had won. He cautioned her, 'It's not over yet.' Indeed it wasn't.

Composing himself, Rocca stroked his putt. The ball raced through the valley, climbed to the upper level of the green and dived into the cup. The roar of the gallery must have been heard through the town. Rocca fell to the ground and buried his face in the turf while he pounded the green with his fists. Then he covered his head with his arms and lay there while the gallery continued cheering. When he stood, he seemed to have tears in his eyes.

Daly, meantime, picked up his putter and walked to the practice green.

Brooks had been watching the finish on television in the R and A clubhouse. When Rocca's putt fell, he rushed out, nearly bumping into one of the R and A's more nimble-footed members, and found Daly. John had lost his yardage book. Brooks gave him his, and both Brad Faxon and Corey Pavin told Daly, 'Go get him.'

The play-off, scheduled for the first, second, 17th and 18th holes, ended almost as soon as it began. Rocca putted six feet past the cup on the first and missed coming back, and then Daly holed from about 30 feet on the second, opening his lead to two strokes.

Evidently assuring he wouldn't finish in the road again on the 17th, Rocca dropped his second shot into the Road Bunker, and took three to get out. He scored a 7 against Daly's immaculate 4. It was the eighth score of 7 or higher for the week on the most difficult hole of the Old Course. With Rocca five strokes behind now, the 18th had turned into nothing more than the quickest route back to the clubhouse.

Daly had become the first American to have won the Open since Mark Calcavecchia had won a play-off at Royal Troon six years earlier, the 11th to have won the oldest championship in golf since Arnold Palmer began the modern crusade in 1960, and the sixth to have won at St Andrews. He was just aged 29 in July of 1995 and could expect 10 more years of golf at the highest level. It was up to him.

FOURTH ROUND RESULTS

HOLE	1	2	3	4	5	6	7	8	9	10	11	12	13	14	15	16	17	18	
PAR	4	4	4	4	5	4	4	3	4	4	3	4	4	5	4	4	4	4	TOTAL
John Daly	4	4	4	3	5	4	3	2	4	4	3	4	4	5	4	5	5	4	71-282
	4	3															4	4	15
Costantino Rocca	4	4	4	4	5	4	5	4	4	5	3	4	4	4	4	4	4	3	73-282
	5	4															7	3	19
Steven Bottomley	4	4	4	3	4	4	4	4	3	4	3	4	4	5	3	4	5	3	69-283
Mark Brooks	4	3	4	4	5	4	4	3	4	4	4	4	4	4	3	6	4	3	71-283
Michael Campbell	4	4	4	4	6	5	4	4	4	4	4	4	4	5	5	4	4	3	76-283
Vijay Singh	4	4	4	4	4	4	4	3	4	4	3	4	5	4	4	4	4	4	71-284
Steve Elkington	5	4	4	5	5	5	3	3	4	4	2	4	4	5	4	4	5	4	74-284
Mark James	5	4	4	3	4	3	5	2	3	4	3	4	5	5	4	4	4	4	70-285
Bob Estes	4	4	5	4	4	4	5	3	3	5	4	3	4	5	3	4	5	3	72-285
Corey Pavin	4	5	4	4	5	5	5	4	3	5	3	3	4	4	4	5	3	4	74-285

HOLE SUMMARY

HOLE	PAR	EAGLES	BIRDIES	PARS	BOGEYS	HIGHER	RANK	AVERAGE
1	4	0	13	79	11	0	14	3.98
2	4	0	9	71	21	2	7	4.16
3	4	0	20	73	10	0	16	3.90
4	4	0	8	79	16	0	12	4.08
5	5	0	45	48	9	1	17	4.68
6	4	0	10	71	21	1	11	4.13
7	4	0	10	65	28	0	6	4.17
8	3	0	5	61	35	2	3	3.33
9	4	0	12	80	9	2	13	4.01
OUT	36	0	132	627	160	8		36.44
10	4	0	8	74	19	2	9	4.15
11	3	0	4	51	43	5	2	3.49
12	4	0	12	65	24	2	7	4.16
13	4	0	13	57	33	0	5	4.19
14	5	0	25	61	16	1	15	4.93
15	4	0	9	72	21	1	10	4.14
16	4	0	4	63	33	3	4	4.34
17	4	0	3	36	54	10	1	4.72
18	4	0	34	67	2	0	18	3.69
IN	36	0	112	546	245	24		37.81
TOTAL	72	0	244	1173	405	32		74.25

Players Below Par	17
Players At Par	9
Players Above Par	77

LOW SCORES

Low First Nine	John Daly	33
	Ross Drummond	33
	Mark James	33
	Peter Senior	33
Low Second Nine	Ryoken Kawagishi	33
Low Round	Ryoken Kawagishi	68

CHAMPIONSHIP HOLE SUMMARY

HOLE	PAR	YARDS	EAGLES	BIRDIES	PARS	BOGEYS	HIGHER	RANK	AVERAGE
1	4	370	1	75	364	75	8	11	4.03
2	4	411	0	47	335	117	24	6	4.23
3	4	371	0	115	359	46	3	16	3.88
4	4	463	0	22	347	144	10	5	4.27
5	5	564	2	152	296	57	16	14	4.88
6	4	416	0	41	351	122	9	8	4.19
7	4	372	0	68	354	95	6	9	4.07
8	3	178	0	30	341	147	5	3	3.24
9	4	356	2	102	353	59	7	13	3.94
OUT	36	3501	5	652	3100	862	88		36.73
10	4	342	0	66	383	66	8	11	4.03
11	3	172	0	31	293	175	24	2	3.38
12	4	316	5	132	312	66	8	15	3.89
13	4	425	0	41	305	157	20	4	4.31
14	5	567	14	201	255	45	8	17	4.69
15	4	413	0	60	389	68	6	10	4.04
16	4	382	0	40	341	132	10	7	4.22
17	4	461	0	13	233	229	48	1	4.62
18	4	354	1	189	305	26	1	18	3.69
IN	36	3432	20	773	2816	964	133		36.87
TOTAL 72		6933	25	1425	5916	1826	221		73.60

	FIRST ROUND	SECOND ROUND	THIRD ROUND	FOURTH ROUND	TOTAL
Players Below Par	59	35	24	17	135
Players At Par	25	20	15	9	69
Players Above Par	75	102	64	77	318

ATTENDANCE

PRACTICE ROUNDS	36,000
FIRST ROUND	32,000
SECOND ROUND	40,000
THIRD ROUND	36,000
FOURTH ROUND	36,000
TOTAL	180,000

John Daly credited his wife, Paulette, as being an inspiration to him during his recent struggles.

COMMENTARY

A CHAMPION OF THE PEOPLE

BY JOHN HOPKINS

Shut your eyes for a moment and think of the new Open champion at work. The images of John Daly on a golf course that come into the mind's eye are of that windblown carpet of blond hair, which looks as though the barber has attended to the upper locks, gone off for a cup of tea and forgotten to return; of the blood red shaft of his driver and the clubhead that seems as big as a blacksmith's anvil; of his massive body turn and how his clubhead points to the ground at the top of the backswing and at the conclusion of his follow-through; of the enormous distances he hits the ball.

These images are as accurate a representation of Daly's idiosyncrasies as Arnold Palmer's hitch of his trousers, the nervous cough of Severiano Ballesteros and the way Jack Nicklaus moves his head to the right before he begins his backswing. The images of Daly are powerful and going to be impressed on us again and again because not only Daly's life but golf itself may never be quite the same after the events that took place on Sunday 24 July 1995. Daly has long been the hero of the people, just about the biggest draw and the biggest name in the game. It was appropriate that he won his Open on the people's golf course, the one Open venue that is not the closely guarded prerogative of its members.

Daly won the Open playing his own style of golf. He hit the ball massive distances, maintaining his composure even when his ball failed to behave as all visible evidence suggested it should, and by demonstrating that he has the imagination to conjure up delicate shots and the game to play them. Though short drinks were a weakness for Daly until he became a teetotaller in 1993, the short game never presented him with any difficulties.

The moment Daly demonstrated this best came on Saturday afternoon after he had hit his last drive of the day to the foot of the stone steps leading from the course to the clubhouse of the Royal and Ancient Golf Club. Daly did not take long to make up his mind which club to play. A brief consultation with Greg Rita, his caddie, and his putter was pulled out of his bag. As the townspeople saw what was about to happen, their hearts went out to the 29-year-old American. They saw a man who had worked out how to play St Andrews and they applauded him. A few claps at first slowly turned into a wholehearted gesture of approval. If Daly wins another Open at St Andrews and after that becomes such a favourite so that he receives accolades from the university of the town, then it may be traced back to this moment. The moment Daly showed humiliation and understanding of the game as it is played at St Andrews.

Daly and the Old Course seem perfectly matched for one another. During an Alfred Dunhill Cup, Michael Bonallack, secretary of the R and A, noted how Daly hit the ball from right to left and has such an inventive and imaginative short game and predicted victory for him in the Open. There was only one proviso and that was whether Daly's patience was good enough on a course where patience would be tested more than any other.

Daly proved it was. In his 72 holes he had 17 birdies, seven bogeys and two double bogeys; and after the first double bogey, which came at the fifth hole on Friday, he covered the remaining 13 holes in three under par, and after the second double bogey, which came on the 17th in the third round, he hit back immediately, scoring a birdie 3 on the 18th.

For these four days, Daly was able to drive the ball where he wanted and to deal with the long putts demanded by the massive greens of the Old Course. His driving on the opening holes on Saturday, when the wind was coming at him over his left shoulder, was prodigious, averaging over 300 yards. It was accurate, too. The soundness of his putting bears out one of the sayings of golf, namely that the men who have the power of a rocket launcher surprisingly

Daly proved to be a favourite at St Andrews.

often also have the touch of a surgeon.

The crowning of John Daly may have taken place just before eight o'clock on a summer's evening when the light was crystal clear and the gusting 45 miles-an-hour wind had dropped to a whisper, but the moments when he demonstrated himself ready to succeed so many famous names in Open history by winning over the Old Course came during Friday's round. Watching an Open is often a hit-and-miss affair — the players hit, the spectators miss. It is easy to take a cup of coffee, a glass of beer or a malt whiskey to a quiet corner and study the next day's play and determine whom to follow. It is less easy to be sure you have elected a match that will prove to be as compelling in reality as it had seemed in prospect.

On Thursday night I studied the order of play for Friday and decided I wanted to watch Daly for a few holes. He was one of four joint leaders with Tom Watson, Ben Crenshaw and Mark McNulty, and I, too, noticed how well Daly had taken to the Old

Course. He bears scrutiny I thought to myself, remembering the vivid picture I had of Daly coming off the course and going straight to the McDonald's stand erected for the Alfred Dunhill Cup and eating several hamburgers while sitting on the wall by the 17th green.

Friday morning dawned clear and sunny, and soon after 8.30 two men watched Daly practise his putting. 'Can Daly win?' one man asked his companion. 'No,' was the response. 'He is not experienced enough. Nor does he have the patience.' Patience and understanding, calmness and inventiveness. These and a sympathetic understanding of what has happened at the Old Course in years gone by are the requirements to score well in an Open on the most famous course in the world. They are as much a key to the Old Course as straight driving is to winning a US Open and nerveless putting is to winning a Masters.

It is time to come clean. I was the man who said Daly could not win, remembering his tendency to give up when out of contention. In the second round of the 1994 Open at Turnberry, for example, he went to the turn in 32, lost a ball on the beach at the 10th, four-putted the 11th for 7 and came home in 40. An 80 in the fourth round gave him sole possession of last place. There was also his pattern of increasingly cavalier play in each round of tournaments on the US Tour earlier this year. While his stroke average for the first two rounds was 71.19 and 70.75, in the third round it rose to 72.82, and 74.36 in the fourth round.

I said to my companion I thought Daly might win an Open at some time but not in 1995. Little did I know that within four hours I was to be converted as Daly demonstrated raw power, self-control, patience and a wonderful touch. The raw power came on the 14th, which he reached with a drive and a six iron, and the 16th where his mighty drive was almost pin-high. He demonstrated self-control by covering the sixth to 18th holes in three under par after squandering two strokes on the par-5 fifth. Inventiveness? How about that deft putt from 25 yards from the flag on the 17th and the 180-foot putt he laid almost stone dead on the 12th green?

By the time he walked off the 18th green he had won me over. John Daly could win the Open I thought, and any doubts that remained were dispelled by a brief chat with Greg Rita. 'On this course he can take advantage of his length,' Rita said. 'Because John hits the ball so far the rest of his game tends to be overlooked. His short game, for example, is underestimated. He is very inventive. Can he win the Open? Of course he can.'

Daly has been a loner since he burst to prominence by winning the 1991 USPGA Championship. To be frank, he was not well regarded by his peers on account of the well-chronicled misdemeanours including excessive drinking, dangerous driving, violence, not to mention the time when he hit a full-blooded drive over the heads of spectators during a clinic. He is not 30 until next April yet Paulette is his third wife, and bore him a daughter a few weeks ago, and he has a young daughter by his second wife, too.

'I was very immature when I won at Crooked Stick,' Daly admitted. 'I am probably pretty immature now, but I was certainly immature then.' The man who had nearly killed himself and his brother by drunken driving swore off the bottle in 1993 and thus has the distinction of winning his first major championship as an alcoholic and his second as a teetotaller.

Daly is his own man, one who shares many of our own failings, and it is because of this that he generates such support. This support could turn him from a rich man into a very rich man over the coming years if he behaves with prudence and grace. In four years Daly has gone from being known as 'Wild Thing,' one who said I 'grip it and rip it,' to the biggest draw in the game. One hopes that one's suspicion about Daly is true — that his excesses off the golf course have ended at the same time as he has become the people's champion on it.

The Old Course suited Daly from the tees, and he also had a subtle touch with his short game.

Arnold Palmer (1961, 1962)

Gary Player (1959, 1968, 1974)

Bob Charles (1963)

Jack Nicklaus (1966, 1970, 1978)

Tom Weiskopf (1973)

Lee Trevino (1971, 1972)

Tom Watson (1975, 1977, 1980, 1982, 1983)

OPEN CHAMPIONSHIP RESULTS

YEAR	CHAMPION	SCORE	MARGIN	RUNNERS-UP	VENUE
1860	Willie Park	174	2	Tom Morris Snr	Prestwick
1861	Tom Morris Snr	163	4	Willie Park	Prestwick
1862	Tom Morris Snr	163	13	Willie Park	Prestwick
1863	Willie Park	168	2	Tom Morris Snr	Prestwick
1864	Tom Morris Snr	167	2	Andrew Strath	Prestwick
1865	Andrew Strath	162	2	Willie Park	Prestwick
1866	Willie Park	169	2	David Park	Prestwick
1867	Tom Morris Snr	170	2	Willie Park	Prestwick
1868	Tom Morris Jnr	157	2	Robert Andrew	Prestwick
1869	Tom Morris Jnr	154	3	Tom Morris Snr	Prestwick
1870	Tom Morris Jnr	149	12	Bob Kirk, David Strath	Prestwick
1871	*No Competition*				
1872	Tom Morris Jnr	166	3	David Strath	Prestwick
1873	Tom Kidd	179	1	Jamie Anderson	St Andrews
1874	Mungo Park	159	2	Tom Morris Jnr	Musselburgh
1875	Willie Park	166	2	Bob Martin	Prestwick
1876	Bob Martin	176	—	David Strath	St Andrews
				(Martin was awarded the title when Strath refused to play-off)	
1877	Jamie Anderson	160	2	Bob Pringle	Musselburgh
1878	Jamie Anderson	157	2	Bob Kirk	Prestwick
1879	Jamie Anderson	169	3	James Allan, Andrew Kirkaldy	St Andrews
1880	Bob Ferguson	162	5	Peter Paxton	Musselburgh
1881	Bob Ferguson	170	3	Jamie Anderson	Prestwick
1882	Bob Ferguson	171	3	Willie Fernie	St Andrews
1883	Willie Fernie	159	Play-off	Bob Ferguson	Musselburgh
				(Fernie won play-off 158 to 159)	
1884	Jack Simpson	160	4	David Rollan, Willie Fernie	Prestwick
1885	Bob Martin	171	1	Archie Simpson	St Andrews
1886	David Brown	157	2	Willie Campbell	Musselburgh
1887	Willie Park Jnr	161	1	Bob Martin	Prestwick
1888	Jack Burns	171	1	David Anderson Jnr, Ben Sayers	St Andrews
1889	Willie Park Jnr	155	Play-off	Andrew Kirkaldy	Musselburgh
				(Park won play-off 158 to 163)	
1890	*John Ball	164	3	Willie Fernie, Archie Simpson	Prestwick
1891	Hugh Kirkaldy	166	2	Willie Fernie, Andrew Kirkaldy	St Andrews
(From 1892 the competition was extended to 72 holes)					
1892	*Harold Hilton	305	3	*John Ball Jnr, James Kirkaldy, Sandy Herd	Muirfield
1893	Willie Auchterlonie	322	2	*Johnny Laidlay	Prestwick

93

YEAR	CHAMPION	SCORE	MARGIN	RUNNERS-UP	VENUE
1894	J.H. Taylor	326	5	Douglas Rolland	Sandwich
1895	J.H. Taylor	322	4	Sandy Herd	St Andrews
1896	Harry Vardon	316	Play-off	J.H. Taylor	Muirfield
				(Vardon won play-off 157 to 161)	
1897	*Harold H. Hilton	314	1	James Braid	Hoylake
1898	Harry Vardon	307	1	Willie Park	Prestwick
1899	Harry Vardon	310	5	Jack White	Sandwich
1900	J.H. Taylor	309	8	Harry Vardon	St Andrews
1901	James Braid	309	3	Harry Vardon	Muirfield
1902	Sandy Herd	307	1	Harry Vardon, James Braid	Hoylake
1903	Harry Vardon	300	6	Tom Vardon	Prestwick
1904	Jack White	296	1	James Braid, J.H. Taylor	Sandwich
1905	James Braid	318	5	J.H. Taylor, R. Jones	St Andrews
1906	James Braid	300	4	J.H. Taylor	Muirfield
1907	Arnaud Massy	312	2	J.H. Taylor	Hoylake
1908	James Braid	291	8	Tom Ball	Prestwick
1909	J.H. Taylor	295	4	James Braid	Deal
1910	James Braid	299	4	Sandy Herd	St Andrews
1911	Harry Vardon	303	Play-off	Arnaud Massy	Sandwich
				(Play-off; Massy conceded at the 35th hole)	
1912	Ted Ray	295	4	Harry Vardon	Muirfield
1913	J.H. Taylor	304	8	Ted Ray	Hoylake
1914	Harry Vardon	306	3	J.H. Taylor	Prestwick
1915-1919 *No Championship*					
1920	George Duncan	303	2	Sandy Herd	Deal
1921	Jock Hutchison	296	Play-off	*Roger Wethered	St Andrews
				(Hutchison won play-off 150 to 159)	
1922	Walter Hagen	300	1	George Duncan, Jim Barnes	Sandwich
1923	Arthur G. Havers	295	1	Walter Hagen	Troon
1924	Walter Hagen	301	1	Ernest Whitcombe	Hoylake
1925	Jim Barnes	300	1	Archie Compston, Ted Ray	Prestwick
1926	*Robert T. Jones Jnr	291	2	Al Watrous	Royal Lytham
1927	*Robert T. Jones Jnr	285	6	Aubrey Boomer, Fred Robson	St Andrews
1928	Walter Hagen	292	2	Gene Sarazen	Sandwich
1929	Walter Hagen	292	6	John Farrell	Muirfield
1930	*Robert T. Jones Jnr	291	2	Leo Diegel, Macdonald Smith	Hoylake
1931	Tommy Armour	296	1	Jose Jurado	Carnoustie
1932	Gene Sarazen	283	5	Macdonald Smith	Prince's
1933	Densmore Shute	292	Play-off	Craig Wood	St Andrews
				(Shute won play-off 149 to 154)	
1934	Henry Cotton	283	5	Sid Brews	Sandwich
1935	Alf Perry	283	4	Alf Padgham	Muirfield
1936	Alf Padgham	287	1	Jimmy Adams	Hoylake
1937	Henry Cotton	290	2	Reg Whitcombe	Carnoustie
1938	Reg Whitcombe	295	2	Jimmy Adams	Sandwich
1939	Richard Burton	290	2	Johnny Bulla	St Andrews
1940-1945 *No Championship*					
1946	Sam Snead	290	4	Bobby Locke, Johnny Bulla	St Andrews
1947	Fred Daly	293	1	Reg Horne, *Frank Stranahan	Hoylake
1948	Henry Cotton	284	5	Fred Daly	Muirfield
1949	Bobby Locke	283	Play-off	Harry Bradshaw	Sandwich
				(Locke won play-off 135 to 147)	
1950	Bobby Locke	279	2	Roberto de Vicenzo	Troon
1951	Max Faulkner	285	2	Tony Cerda	Royal Portrush
1952	Bobby Locke	287	1	Peter Thomson	Royal Lytham
1953	Ben Hogan	282	4	*Frank Stranahan, Dai Rees, Peter Thomson, Tony Cerda	Carnoustie

YEAR	CHAMPION	SCORE	MARGIN	RUNNERS-UP	VENUE
1954	Peter Thomson	283	1	Sid Scott, Dai Rees, Bobby Locke	Royal Birkdale
1955	Peter Thomson	281	2	Johnny Fallon	St Andrews
1956	Peter Thomson	286	3	Flory van Donck	Hoylake
1957	Bobby Locke	279	3	Peter Thomson	St Andrews
1958	Peter Thomson	278	Play-off	David Thomas	Royal Lytham
				(Thomson won play-off 139 to 143)	
1959	Gary Player	284	2	Flory van Donck, Fred Bullock	Muirfield
1960	Kel Nagle	278	1	Arnold Palmer	St Andrews
1961	Arnold Palmer	284	1	Dai Rees	Royal Birkdale
1962	Arnold Palmer	276	6	Kel Nagle	Troon
1963	Bob Charles	277	Play-off	Phil Rodgers	Royal Lytham
				(Charles won play-off 140 to 148)	
1964	Tony Lema	279	5	Jack Nicklaus	St Andrews
1965	Peter Thomson	285	2	Christy O'Connor, Brian Huggett	Royal Birkdale
1966	Jack Nicklaus	282	1	David Thomas, Doug Sanders	Muirfield
1967	Roberto de Vicenzo	278	2	Jack Nicklaus	Hoylake
1968	Gary Player	289	2	Jack Nicklaus, Bob Charles	Carnoustie
1969	Tony Jacklin	280	2	Bob Charles	Royal Lytham
1970	Jack Nicklaus	283	Play-off	Doug Sanders	St Andrews
				(Nicklaus won play-off 72 to 73)	
1971	Lee Trevino	278	1	Lu Liang Huan	Royal Birkdale
1972	Lee Trevino	278	1	Jack Nicklaus	Muirfield
1973	Tom Weiskopf	276	3	Neil Coles, Johnny Miller	Troon
1974	Gary Player	282	4	Peter Oosterhuis	Royal Lytham
1975	Tom Watson	279	Play-off	Jack Newton	Carnoustie
				(Watson won play-off 71 to 72)	
1976	Johnny Miller	279	6	Jack Nicklaus, Severiano Ballesteros	Royal Birkdale
1977	Tom Watson	268	1	Jack Nicklaus	Turnberry
1978	Jack Nicklaus	281	2	Simon Owen, Ben Crenshaw,	St Andrews
				Raymond Floyd, Tom Kite	
1979	Severiano Ballesteros	283	3	Jack Nicklaus, Ben Crenshaw	Royal Lytham
1980	Tom Watson	271	4	Lee Trevino	Muirfield
1981	Bill Rogers	276	4	Bernhard Langer	Sandwich
1982	Tom Watson	284	1	Peter Oosterhuis, Nick Price	Troon
1983	Tom Watson	275	1	Hale Irwin, Andy Bean	Royal Birkdale
1984	Severiano Ballesteros	276	2	Bernhard Langer, Tom Watson	St Andrews
1985	Sandy Lyle	282	1	Payne Stewart	Sandwich
1986	Greg Norman	280	5	Gordon J. Brand	Turnberry
1987	Nick Faldo	279	1	Rodger Davis, Paul Azinger	Muirfield
1988	Severiano Ballesteros	273	2	Nick Price	Royal Lytham
1989	Mark Calcavecchia	275	Play-off	Greg Norman, Wayne Grady	Royal Troon
				(Calcavecchia won four-hole play-off)	
1990	Nick Faldo	270	5	Mark McNulty, Payne Stewart	St Andrews
1991	Ian Baker-Finch	272	2	Mike Harwood	Royal Birkdale
1992	Nick Faldo	272	1	John Cook	Muirfield
1993	Greg Norman	267	2	Nick Faldo	Sandwich
1994	Nick Price	268	1	Jesper Parnevik	Turnberry
1995	John Daly	282	Play-off	Costantino Rocca	St Andrews
				(Daly won four-hole play-off)	

*Denotes amateurs

Seve Ballesteros (1979, 1984, 1988)

Sandy Lyle (1985)

Mark Calcavecchia (1989)

Nick Faldo (1987, 1990, 1992)

Nick Price (1994)

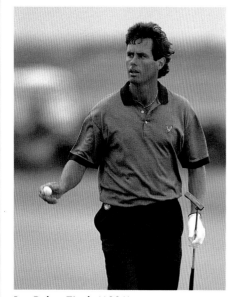

Ian Baker-Finch (1991)

Greg Norman (1986, 1993)

OPEN CHAMPIONSHIP RECORDS

MOST VICTORIES
6, Harry Vardon, 1896-98-99-1903-11-14
5, James Braid, 1901-05-06-08-10; J.H. Taylor, 1894-95-1900-09-13; Peter Thomson, 1954-55-56-58-65; Tom Watson, 1975-77-80-82-83

MOST TIMES RUNNER-UP OR JOINT RUNNER-UP
7, Jack Nicklaus, 1964-67-68-72-76-77-79
6, J.H. Taylor, 1896-1904-05-06-07-14

OLDEST WINNER
Old Tom Morris, 46 years 99 days, 1867
Roberto de Vicenzo, 44 years 93 days, 1967

YOUNGEST WINNER
Young Tom Morris, 17 years 5 months 8 days, 1868
Willie Auchterlonie, 21 years 24 days, 1893
Severiano Ballesteros, 22 years 3 months 12 days, 1979

YOUNGEST AND OLDEST COMPETITOR
John Ball, 14 years, 1878
Gene Sarazen, 71 years 4 months 13 days, 1973

BIGGEST MARGIN OF VICTORY
13 strokes, Old Tom Morris, 1862
12 strokes, Young Tom Morris, 1870
8 strokes, J.H. Taylor, 1900 and 1913; James Braid, 1908
6 strokes, Bobby Jones, 1927; Walter Hagen, 1929; Arnold Palmer, 1962; Johnny Miller, 1976

LOWEST WINNING AGGREGATES
267 (66, 68, 69, 64), Greg Norman, Royal St George's, 1993
268 (68, 70, 65, 65), Tom Watson, Turnberry, 1977; (69, 66, 67, 66), Nick Price, Turnberry, 1994
270 (67, 65, 67, 71), Nick Faldo, St Andrews, 1990
271 (68, 70, 64, 69), Tom Watson, Muirfield, 1980

LOWEST AGGREGATES BY RUNNER-UP
269 (68, 70, 65, 66), Jack Nicklaus, Turnberry, 1977; (69, 63, 70, 67), Nick Faldo, Royal St George's, 1993; (68, 66, 68, 67), Jesper Parnevik, Turnberry, 1994
273 (66, 67, 70, 70), John Cook, Muirfield, 1992

LOWEST AGGREGATE BY AN AMATEUR
281 (68, 72, 70, 71), Iain Pyman, Royal St George's, 1993

LOWEST INDIVIDUAL ROUND
63, Mark Hayes, second round, Turnberry, 1977; Isao Aoki, third round, Muirfield, 1980; Greg Norman, second round, Turnberry, 1986; Paul Broadhurst, third round, St Andrews, 1990; Jodie Mudd, fourth round, Royal Birkdale, 1991; Nick Faldo, second round, and Payne Stewart, fourth round, Royal St George's, 1993

LOWEST INDIVIDUAL ROUND BY AN AMATEUR
66, Frank Stranahan, fourth round, Troon, 1950

LOWEST FIRST ROUND
64, Craig Stadler, Royal Birkdale, 1983; Christy O'Connor Jr., Royal St George's, 1985; Rodger Davis, Muirfield, 1987; Raymond Floyd and Steve Pate, Muirfield, 1992

LOWEST SECOND ROUND
63, Mark Hayes, Turnberry, 1977; Greg Norman, Turnberry, 1986; Nick Faldo, Royal St George's, 1993

LOWEST THIRD ROUND
63, Isao Aoki, Muirfield, 1980; Paul Broadhurst, St Andrews, 1990

LOWEST FOURTH ROUND
63, Jodie Mudd, Royal Birkdale, 1991; Payne Stewart, Royal St George's, 1993

LOWEST FIRST 36 HOLES
130 (66, 64), Nick Faldo, Muirfield, 1992
132 (67, 65), Henry Cotton, Sandwich, 1934; (66, 66), Greg Norman and (67, 65), Nick Faldo, St Andrews, 1990; (69, 63), Nick Faldo, Royal St George's, 1993

LOWEST SECOND 36 HOLES
130 (65, 65), Tom Watson, Turnberry, 1977; (64, 66), Ian Baker-Finch, Royal Birkdale, 1991; (66, 64), Anders Forsbrand, Turnberry, 1994

LOWEST FIRST 54 HOLES
199 (67, 65, 67), Nick Faldo, St Andrews, 1990; (66, 64, 69), Nick Faldo, Muirfield, 1992

LOWEST FINAL 54 HOLES
199 (66, 67, 66), Nick Price, Turnberry, 1994
200 (70, 65, 65), Tom Watson, Turnberry, 1977; (63, 70, 67), Nick Faldo, Royal St George's, 1993; (66, 64, 70), Fuzzy Zoeller, Turnberry, 1994; (66, 70, 64), Nick Faldo, Turnberry, 1994

LOWEST 9 HOLES
28, Denis Durnian, first 9, Royal Birkdale, 1983
29, Peter Thomson and Tom Haliburton, first 9, Royal Lytham, 1958; Tony Jacklin, first 9, St Andrews, 1970; Bill Longmuir, first 9, Royal Lytham, 1979; David J. Russell, first 9, Royal Lytham, 1988; Ian Baker-Finch and Paul Broadhurst, first 9, St Andrews, 1990; Ian Baker-Finch, first 9, Royal Birkdale, 1991

CHAMPIONS IN THREE DECADES
Harry Vardon, 1896, 1903, 1911
J.H. Taylor, 1894, 1900, 1913
Gary Player, 1959, 1968, 1974

BIGGEST SPAN BETWEEN FIRST AND LAST VICTORIES
19 years, J.H. Taylor, 1894-1913
18 years, Harry Vardon, 1896-1914
15 years, Gary Player, 1959-74
14 years, Henry Cotton, 1934-48

SUCCESSIVE VICTORIES
4, Young Tom Morris, 1868-72. No championship in 1871
3, Jamie Anderson, 1877-79; Bob Ferguson, 1880-82, Peter Thomson, 1954-56
2, Old Tom Morris, 1861-62; J.H. Taylor, 1894-95; Harry Vardon, 1898-99; James Braid, 1905-06; Bobby Jones, 1926-27; Walter Hagen, 1928-29; Bobby Locke, 1949-50; Arnold Palmer, 1961-62; Lee Trevino, 1971-72; Tom Watson, 1982-83

VICTORIES BY AMATEURS
3, Bobby Jones, 1926-27-30
2, Harold Hilton, 1892-97
1, John Ball, 1890
Roger Wethered lost a play-off in 1921

HIGHEST NUMBER OF TOP FIVE FINISHES
16, J.H. Taylor, Jack Nicklaus
15, Harry Vardon, James Braid

HIGHEST NUMBER OF ROUNDS UNDER 70
31, Jack Nicklaus
30, Nick Faldo
27, Tom Watson
21, Lee Trevino
20, Greg Norman, Severiano Ballesteros
18, Nick Price
16, Bernhard Langer
15, Peter Thomson, Gary Player
14, Ben Crenshaw

OUTRIGHT LEADER AFTER EVERY ROUND
Willie Auchterlonie, 1893; J.H. Taylor, 1894 and 1900; James Braid, 1908; Ted Ray, 1912; Bobby Jones, 1927; Gene Sarazen, 1932; Henry Cotton, 1934; Tom Weiskopf, 1973

RECORD LEADS (SINCE 1892)
After 18 holes:
4 strokes, James Braid, 1908; Bobby Jones, 1927; Henry Cotton, 1934; Christy O'Connor Jr., 1985

After 36 holes:
9 strokes, Henry Cotton, 1934
After 54 holes:
10 strokes, Henry Cotton, 1934
7 strokes, Tony Lema, 1964
6 strokes, James Braid, 1908
5 strokes, Arnold Palmer, 1962; Bill Rogers, 1981; Nick Faldo, 1990

CHAMPIONS WITH EACH ROUND LOWER THAN PREVIOUS ONE
Jack White, 1904, Sandwich, (80, 75, 72, 69)
James Braid, 1906, Muirfield, (77, 76, 74, 73)
Ben Hogan, 1953, Carnoustie, (73, 71, 70, 68)
Gary Player, 1959, Muirfield, (75, 71, 70, 68)

CHAMPION WITH FOUR ROUNDS THE SAME
Densmore Shute, 1933, St Andrews, (73, 73, 73, 73) (excluding the play-off)

BIGGEST VARIATION BETWEEN ROUNDS OF A CHAMPION
14 strokes, Henry Cotton, 1934, second round 65, fourth round 79
11 strokes, Jack White, 1904, first round 80, fourth round 69; Greg Norman, 1986, first round 74, second round 63, third round 74

BIGGEST VARIATION BETWEEN TWO ROUNDS
17 strokes, Jack Nicklaus, 1981, first round 83, second round 66; Ian Baker-Finch, 1986, first round 86, second round 69

BEST COMEBACK BY CHAMPIONS
After 18 holes:
Harry Vardon, 1896, 11 strokes behind the leader
After 36 holes:
George Duncan, 1920, 13 strokes behind the leader
After 54 holes:
Jim Barnes, 1925, 5 strokes behind the leader
Of non-champions, Greg Norman, 1989, 7 strokes behind the leader and lost in a play-off

CHAMPIONS WITH FOUR ROUNDS UNDER 70
Greg Norman, 1993, Royal St George's, (66, 68, 69, 64); Nick Price, 1994, Turnberry, (69, 66, 67, 66)
Of non-champions:
Ernie Els, 1993, Royal St George's, (68, 69, 69, 68); Jesper Parnevik, 1994, Turnberry, (68, 66, 68, 67)

BEST FINISHING ROUND BY A CHAMPION
64, Greg Norman, Royal St George's, 1993
65, Tom Watson, Turnberry, 1977; Severiano Ballesteros, Royal Lytham, 1988
66, Johnny Miller, Royal Birkdale, 1976; Ian Baker-Finch, Royal Birkdale, 1991; Nick Price, Turnberry, 1994

WORST FINISHING ROUND BY A CHAMPION SINCE 1920
79, Henry Cotton, Sandwich, 1934
78, Reg Whitcombe, Sandwich, 1938
77, Walter Hagen, Hoylake, 1924

WORST OPENING ROUND BY A CHAMPION SINCE 1919

80, George Duncan, Deal, 1920 (he also had a second round of 80)

77, Walter Hagen, Hoylake, 1924

BEST OPENING ROUND BY A CHAMPION

66, Peter Thomson, Royal Lytham, 1958; Nick Faldo, Muirfield, 1992; Greg Norman, Royal St George's, 1993

67, Henry Cotton, Sandwich, 1934; Tom Watson, Royal Birkdale, 1983; Severiano Ballesteros, Royal Lytham, 1988; Nick Faldo, St Andrews, 1990; John Daly, St Andrews, 1995

BIGGEST RECOVERY IN 18 HOLES BY A CHAMPION

George Duncan, Deal, 1920, was 13 strokes behind the leader, Abe Mitchell, after 36 holes and level after 54

MOST APPEARANCES ON FINAL DAY (SINCE 1892)

30, J.H. Taylor, Jack Nicklaus

27, Harry Vardon, James Braid

26, Peter Thomson, Gary Player

23, Dai Rees

22, Henry Cotton

CHAMPIONSHIP WITH HIGHEST NUMBER OF ROUNDS UNDER 70

148, Turnberry, 1994

CHAMPIONSHIP SINCE 1946 WITH THE FEWEST ROUNDS UNDER 70

St Andrews, 1946; Hoylake, 1947; Portrush, 1951; Hoylake, 1956; Carnoustie, 1968. All had only two rounds under 70

LONGEST COURSE

Carnoustie, 1968, 7252 yd (6631 m)

COURSES MOST OFTEN USED

St Andrews, 25; Prestwick, 24; Muirfield, 14; Sandwich, 12; Hoylake, 10; Royal Lytham, 8; Royal Birkdale, 7; Musselburgh, and Royal Troon, 6; Carnoustie, 5; Turnberry, 3; Deal, 2; Royal Portrush and Prince's, 1

PRIZE MONEY

Year	Total	First Prize
1860	nil	nil
1863	10	nil
1864	16	6
1876	27	10
1889	22	8
1891	28.50	10
1892	110	(Amateur winner)
1893	100	30
1910	125	50
1920	225	75
1927	275	100
1930	400	100
1931	500	100
1946	1,000	150
1949	1,700	300
1953	2,450	500
1954	3,500	750
1955	3,750	1,000
1958	4,850	1,000
1959	5,000	1,000
1960	7,000	1,250
1961	8,500	1,400
1963	8,500	1,500
1965	10,000	1,750
1966	15,000	2,100
1968	20,000	3,000
1969	30,000	4,250
1970	40,000	5,250
1971	45,000	5,500
1972	50,000	5,500
1975	75,000	7,500
1977	100,000	10,000
1978	125,000	12,500
1979	155,000	15,500
1980	200,000	25,000
1982	250,000	32,000
1983	300,000	40,000
1984	451,000	55,000
1985	530,000	65,000
1986	600,000	70,000
1987	650,000	75,000
1988	700,000	80,000
1989	750,000	80,000
1990	825,000	85,000
1991	900,000	90,000
1992	950,000	95,000
1993	1,000,000	100,000
1994	1,100,000	110,000
1995	1,250,000	125,000

ATTENDANCE

Year	Attendance
1962	37,098
1963	24,585
1964	35,954
1965	32,927
1966	40,182
1967	29,880
1968	51,819
1969	46,001
1970	81,593
1971	70,076
1972	84,746
1973	78,810
1974	92,796
1975	85,258
1976	92,021
1977	87,615
1978	125,271
1979	134,501
1980	131,610
1981	111,987
1982	133,299
1983	142,892
1984	193,126
1985	141,619
1986	134,261
1987	139,189
1988	191,334
1989	160,639
1990	208,680
1991	189,435
1992	146,427
1993	141,000
1994	128,000
1995	180,000

COMPLETE SCORES OF 124TH OPEN CHAMPIONSHIP

*Denotes amateurs

HOLE		1	2	3	4	5	6	7	8	9	10	11	12	13	14	15	16	17	18	TOTAL
PAR		4	4	4	4	5	4	4	3	4	4	3	4	4	5	4	4	4	4	TOTAL
John Daly	Round 1	4	4	3	3	4	5	4	4	3	4	3	3	4	4	4	4	4	3	67
	Round 2	4	4	4	4	7	4	4	3	4	3	2	3	5	4	4	4	4	4	71
	Round 3	5	4	4	4	5	4	4	4	3	4	3	3	4	4	5	4	6	3	73
	Round 4	4	4	4	3	5	4	3	2	4	4	3	4	4	5	4	5	5	4	71-282
	Play-off	4	3															4	4	15
Costantino Rocca	Round 1	3	5	4	4	4	4	4	2	4	3	2	5	5	5	3	4	4	4	69
	Round 2	4	3	4	4	4	4	3	3	4	4	3	5	4	5	4	4	5	3	70
	Round 3	4	3	4	4	5	4	4	4	4	4	3	2	4	4	4	5	4	4	70
	Round 4	4	4	4	4	5	4	5	4	4	5	3	4	4	4	4	4	4	3	73-282
	Play-off	5	4															7	3	19
Steven Bottomley	Round 1	3	4	4	4	5	4	4	3	4	3	3	4	4	5	4	4	4	4	70
	Round 2	4	5	4	4	6	4	4	3	4	4	3	4	4	4	4	4	4	3	72
	Round 3	4	5	4	5	5	4	4	3	4	4	2	4	4	4	4	4	5	3	72
	Round 4	4	4	4	3	4	4	4	4	3	4	3	4	4	5	3	4	5	3	69-283
Mark Brooks	Round 1	4	3	4	4	5	4	4	3	4	4	3	4	4	4	4	4	5	3	70
	Round 2	3	4	4	4	4	5	4	3	3	5	2	4	4	4	4	5	4	3	69
	Round 3	4	5	4	4	5	5	4	3	5	4	4	4	4	4	4	4	3	3	73
	Round 4	4	3	4	4	5	4	4	3	4	4	4	4	4	4	3	6	4	3	71-283
Michael Campbell	Round 1	4	4	3	4	5	5	4	3	4	4	3	5	3	5	4	4	4	3	71
	Round 2	3	4	4	5	5	4	4	3	5	4	4	3	4	5	3	3	5	3	71
	Round 3	4	4	3	4	4	4	3	3	3	4	3	3	3	4	4	4	4	4	65
	Round 4	4	4	4	4	6	5	4	4	4	4	4	4	4	5	5	4	4	3	76-283
Vijay Singh	Round 1	4	3	3	4	5	4	3	3	4	5	3	4	4	4	4	4	4	3	68
	Round 2	4	4	4	5	5	4	3	4	4	4	4	3	4	4	4	4	5	3	72
	Round 3	4	5	3	5	5	4	4	4	3	5	3	3	4	4	4	5	4	4	73
	Round 4	4	4	4	4	4	4	4	3	4	4	3	4	5	4	4	4	4	4	71-284
Steve Elkington	Round 1	5	4	4	4	4	4	4	3	4	4	4	4	4	4	3	5	4	4	72
	Round 2	3	6	3	3	5	3	5	3	4	4	3	3	5	4	4	4	4	3	69
	Round 3	3	4	3	4	5	4	4	3	5	4	3	4	3	4	4	4	5	3	69
	Round 4	5	4	4	5	5	5	3	3	4	4	2	4	4	5	4	4	5	4	74-284
Mark James	Round 1	3	6	4	4	5	3	4	4	4	5	3	4	4	4	4	4	4	3	72
	Round 2	4	4	3	4	5	4	5	3	4	4	4	5	4	4	5	5	5	4	75
	Round 3	4	4	4	4	5	4	4	3	4	3	2	3	4	3	5	5	4	3	68
	Round 4	5	4	4	3	4	3	5	2	3	4	3	4	5	5	4	4	4	4	70-285

100

HOLE		1	2	3	4	5	6	7	8	9	10	11	12	13	14	15	16	17	18	
PAR		4	4	4	4	5	4	4	3	4	4	3	4	4	5	4	4	4	4	TOTAL
Bob Estes	Round 1	3	4	4	5	4	4	4	3	4	4	3	5	4	5	4	4	4	4	72
	Round 2	4	3	4	4	4	4	4	3	4	4	4	3	4	4	5	5	4	3	70
	Round 3	4	4	4	5	5	5	4	3	4	4	3	3	4	4	4	5	4	3	71
	Round 4	4	4	5	4	4	4	5	3	3	5	4	3	4	5	3	4	5	3	72-285
Corey Pavin	Round 1	4	4	3	5	4	4	3	3	4	4	3	3	4	4	4	4	5	4	69
	Round 2	4	4	3	4	5	4	4	3	4	3	3	4	4	5	4	5	4	3	70
	Round 3	3	5	4	4	5	4	4	4	4	4	3	4	4	4	4	5	4	3	72
	Round 4	4	5	4	4	5	5	5	4	3	5	3	3	4	4	4	5	3	4	74-285
Payne Stewart	Round 1	3	5	4	5	5	4	3	3	4	3	3	5	5	3	5	4	4	4	72
	Round 2	3	4	4	5	4	4	4	4	4	3	4	3	4	4	3	4	4	3	68
	Round 3	4	4	4	4	7	4	4	3	4	3	2	4	6	7	4	4	3	4	75
	Round 4	3	4	4	5	5	4	3	3	4	5	3	3	4	4	4	4	5	4	71-286
Brett Ogle	Round 1	4	5	5	4	5	4	4	3	4	4	3	4	5	4	5	3	4	3	73
	Round 2	4	4	5	4	4	5	4	3	3	4	4	3	4	4	3	4	4	3	69
	Round 3	5	5	4	5	4	4	4	3	3	3	3	3	5	4	3	5	5	3	71
	Round 4	4	3	4	4	5	5	4	4	5	5	3	4	4	4	3	4	4	4	73-286
Sam Torrance	Round 1	4	3	4	4	5	4	4	3	4	4	4	4	4	4	4	3	5	4	71
	Round 2	4	4	4	4	5	3	4	3	4	4	3	3	5	5	4	4	4	3	70
	Round 3	4	5	4	4	4	5	4	3	4	4	3	4	4	4	4	4	4	3	71
	Round 4	4	4	3	4	5	4	4	4	5	4	3	5	5	5	4	4	4	3	74-286
Ernie Els	Round 1	4	4	4	3	4	4	4	3	5	3	3	4	4	5	4	5	4	4	71
	Round 2	4	3	3	4	5	4	4	3	4	3	3	3	3	4	5	4	5	4	68
	Round 3	5	4	4	4	5	4	4	3	5	4	3	4	5	4	4	3	4	3	72
	Round 4	4	4	4	4	4	5	5	4	4	4	3	4	4	5	4	4	5	4	75-286
Greg Norman	Round 1	4	3	4	4	4	5	4	3	3	4	4	4	4	5	4	5	4	3	71
	Round 2	4	3	4	4	4	4	4	4	5	3	6	4	4	5	4	4	4	4	74
	Round 3	3	4	4	5	5	4	4	4	3	4	3	3	4	4	5	4	4	5	72
	Round 4	4	4	4	4	5	3	4	3	4	4	3	4	4	4	3	5	4	4	70-287
Robert Allenby	Round 1	3	4	4	4	5	4	5	3	4	3	2	4	5	4	4	4	5	4	71
	Round 2	4	4	4	5	5	4	5	3	4	4	3	4	4	5	3	4	5	4	74
	Round 3	4	4	3	4	5	4	4	3	4	4	3	4	4	4	4	4	5	4	71
	Round 4	4	5	4	4	4	4	5	3	4	4	2	5	4	5	3	4	3	4	71-287
Ben Crenshaw	Round 1	4	3	4	5	4	3	3	3	4	4	3	4	4	4	3	4	4	4	67
	Round 2	4	4	3	5	5	4	4	3	4	5	4	3	4	4	4	5	4	3	72
	Round 3	4	4	5	5	4	4	5	3	5	5	3	4	4	5	3	3	6	4	76
	Round 4	4	4	4	4	5	4	4	2	4	4	4	4	5	4	3	4	5	4	72-287
Per-Ulrik Johansson	Round 1	4	3	4	4	4	4	3	3	3	4	4	4	5	5	4	3	4	4	69
	Round 2	4	4	5	4	4	4	4	4	4	5	4	4	5	5	5	4	5	4	78
	Round 3	3	4	3	4	5	4	5	3	3	4	2	3	4	4	4	5	5	3	68
	Round 4	4	4	4	3	4	4	3	4	4	4	3	4	4	6	4	4	5	4	72-287
Brad Faxon	Round 1	4	4	3	4	4	5	4	3	4	4	4	4	4	5	4	4	4	3	71
	Round 2	4	4	3	4	4	4	4	3	4	3	4	3	4	4	4	4	4	3	67
	Round 3	5	4	4	6	5	4	4	2	5	4	4	3	5	4	4	4	4	4	75
	Round 4	4	5	4	4	4	4	4	2	4	4	3	5	5	4	5	5	5	3	74-287
Peter Mitchell	Round 1	4	4	4	5	5	4	4	4	3	4	3	3	4	5	4	5	4	4	73
	Round 2	5	4	4	4	5	4	4	4	3	4	3	5	4	5	4	4	4	4	74
	Round 3	4	4	4	5	5	4	4	3	4	3	3	3	4	4	4	5	4	3	71
	Round 4	4	5	4	4	5	3	3	3	4	3	3	4	3	4	4	5	5	4	70-288

HOLE		1	2	3	4	5	6	7	8	9	10	11	12	13	14	15	16	17	18	
PAR		4	4	4	4	5	4	4	3	4	4	3	4	4	5	4	4	4	4	TOTAL
David Duval	Round 1	4	4	4	4	4	4	4	3	4	3	3	4	4	4	4	4	7	3	71
	Round 2	3	4	3	4	5	4	5	4	5	5	3	4	4	4	4	5	5	5	75
	Round 3	3	5	4	5	5	4	3	2	3	5	4	3	4	5	4	4	4	3	70
	Round 4	4	4	5	4	4	4	4	3	4	4	4	3	4	5	4	4	5	3	72-288
Andrew Coltart	Round 1	3	4	3	5	5	5	5	3	4	3	3	3	3	6	4	4	4	3	70
	Round 2	4	4	4	4	6	4	4	3	4	4	4	4	4	4	4	5	4	4	74
	Round 3	4	4	4	4	5	5	4	3	3	4	3	5	4	3	4	4	5	3	71
	Round 4	3	4	5	3	5	4	4	4	3	4	4	4	4	5	4	5	5	3	73-288
Barry Lane	Round 1	3	5	4	4	4	5	4	4	4	4	3	4	5	4	4	4	4	3	72
	Round 2	3	4	4	5	5	4	6	3	4	5	3	3	4	5	4	3	5	3	73
	Round 3	5	4	4	4	4	4	4	3	4	3	3	3	3	4	4	3	5	4	68
	Round 4	4	5	4	4	5	4	4	4	4	4	4	4	5	5	4	4	4	3	75-288
Lee Janzen	Round 1	4	5	3	4	4	5	4	4	3	4	3	5	4	5	4	4	4	4	73
	Round 2	4	4	4	4	5	4	4	3	5	4	4	3	4	5	4	4	5	3	73
	Round 3	3	5	4	5	4	4	4	3	4	4	3	4	5	4	4	4	4	3	71
	Round 4	4	5	3	5	4	4	4	3	4	4	3	4	3	5	4	5	5	3	72-289
*Steven Webster	Round 1	4	4	4	4	4	4	3	3	4	4	4	4	4	4	4	4	4	4	70
	Round 2	4	4	3	4	3	4	3	3	4	5	4	6	5	4	3	5	4	4	72
	Round 3	4	4	4	4	5	4	3	4	4	4	5	3	4	5	5	4	5	3	74
	Round 4	4	3	4	5	4	4	4	3	4	4	4	4	4	5	4	5	4	4	73-289
Bernhard Langer	Round 1	4	4	3	4	5	4	4	2	4	4	3	4	5	5	4	4	5	4	72
	Round 2	3	5	4	4	5	3	4	4	3	4	3	3	4	5	5	5	4	3	71
	Round 3	5	4	4	5	6	4	4	4	4	3	2	4	4	4	4	4	4	4	73
	Round 4	4	5	4	4	4	3	4	3	4	4	4	4	4	5	4	5	4	4	73-289
Jesper Parnevik	Round 1	4	5	4	4	5	5	4	3	4	4	3	4	5	4	5	4	4	4	75
	Round 2	4	4	4	4	5	4	4	3	4	4	4	4	4	4	4	4	4	3	71
	Round 3	4	4	3	5	5	4	4	3	4	4	3	3	4	5	4	4	4	3	70
	Round 4	4	4	3	4	5	5	3	3	4	4	2	5	5	5	4	4	5	4	73-289
Mark Calcavecchia	Round 1	4	4	4	4	4	3	3	3	4	5	4	4	4	5	4	4	5	3	71
	Round 2	5	4	4	4	5	4	4	3	4	3	3	3	6	5	4	3	5	3	72
	Round 3	4	4	4	5	5	3	4	3	4	4	3	5	4	4	4	4	4	4	72
	Round 4	3	4	3	5	5	6	4	3	4	4	4	4	5	4	4	4	5	3	74-289
Bill Glasson	Round 1	4	4	4	4	5	4	3	3	3	4	4	4	4	4	3	4	4	3	68
	Round 2	4	4	3	4	5	4	4	3	3	4	4	3	4	5	4	4	8	4	74
	Round 3	4	5	3	4	5	3	4	3	4	5	2	3	5	4	5	5	5	3	72
	Round 4	4	4	3	5	5	4	4	3	4	3	4	5	4	5	4	5	6	3	75-289
Katsuyoshi Tomori	Round 1	3	4	3	4	4	4	3	4	4	4	3	4	4	5	4	4	5	4	70
	Round 2	4	4	4	4	4	4	3	3	4	4	3	3	5	4	4	3	4	4	68
	Round 3	4	4	4	5	5	4	5	3	3	4	3	3	4	4	4	5	5	4	73
	Round 4	4	5	3	4	5	4	5	4	6	4	4	4	4	5	4	4	5	4	78-289
Ross Drummond	Round 1	4	4	4	4	4	5	4	4	5	5	3	4	4	4	3	5	4	4	74
	Round 2	4	4	3	4	4	5	4	3	3	3	4	3	5	4	4	4	3	4	68
	Round 3	5	4	4	5	5	4	4	4	4	5	4	4	4	4	4	4	5	4	77
	Round 4	4	3	3	4	5	4	3	3	4	3	3	5	5	5	4	5	4	4	71-290
Jose Maria Olazabal	Round 1	4	4	3	4	5	5	3	3	4	3	3	4	5	5	4	4	5	4	72
	Round 2	4	4	4	4	5	4	3	3	4	4	3	4	4	5	4	4	5	4	72
	Round 3	4	5	4	4	5	6	4	3	4	4	3	3	4	4	4	5	5	3	74
	Round 4	4	4	3	4	5	4	3	3	5	4	4	4	4	4	4	4	5	4	72-290

HOLE		1	2	3	4	5	6	7	8	9	10	11	12	13	14	15	16	17	18	
PAR		4	4	4	4	5	4	4	3	4	4	3	4	4	5	4	4	4	4	TOTAL
David Frost	Round 1	4	4	3	4	4	4	5	3	4	4	3	4	5	4	4	4	5	4	72
	Round 2	4	5	4	4	5	5	4	3	4	3	2	4	4	5	3	4	5	4	72
	Round 3	4	4	4	5	5	4	3	4	4	3	4	3	4	6	5	4	4	4	74
	Round 4	4	3	4	4	4	4	4	4	3	4	5	4	4	5	4	5	4	3	72-290
Hisayuki Sasaki	Round 1	5	4	4	4	5	4	5	3	3	4	3	4	4	5	4	4	5	4	74
	Round 2	4	4	4	5	5	4	4	3	4	4	3	2	4	4	4	4	5	4	71
	Round 3	4	3	4	4	5	4	3	3	2	4	3	4	4	10	3	4	4	4	72
	Round 4	4	5	3	4	6	4	5	3	4	4	3	3	3	5	4	4	5	4	73-290
John Huston	Round 1	4	4	4	4	5	5	3	3	4	3	3	4	5	5	4	3	5	3	71
	Round 2	4	3	4	4	5	4	4	3	4	5	3	4	5	5	5	4	5	3	74
	Round 3	4	4	3	5	6	3	4	4	4	4	3	3	4	5	4	4	4	4	72
	Round 4	4	4	4	4	4	4	4	3	4	4	4	4	5	5	4	4	4	4	73-290
Peter Jacobsen	Round 1	4	3	4	4	4	4	4	2	4	4	3	4	4	5	4	4	6	4	71
	Round 2	5	4	4	4	7	5	4	4	4	4	3	4	5	4	4	4	4	3	76
	Round 3	4	4	4	5	4	4	4	3	4	3	3	3	4	4	4	4	5	4	70
	Round 4	4	4	4	4	4	4	5	3	4	5	4	4	4	4	4	4	4	4	73-290
Darren Clarke	Round 1	4	4	3	3	5	5	5	3	3	3	3	3	5	4	3	4	5	4	69
	Round 2	5	3	5	4	5	4	5	3	3	4	4	4	6	7	4	4	4	3	77
	Round 3	3	4	4	4	5	4	4	3	3	4	3	4	4	5	4	4	5	3	70
	Round 4	4	4	4	4	4	4	4	4	5	4	3	4	4	5	4	4	6	3	74-290
David Feherty	Round 1	3	5	3	4	4	5	3	3	4	4	2	4	4	4	4	4	4	4	68
	Round 2	4	5	4	5	5	4	4	4	4	4	5	3	4	5	4	3	4	4	75
	Round 3	4	4	3	6	5	4	4	3	4	4	3	4	3	4	4	4	5	3	71
	Round 4	3	4	4	4	5	4	4	3	4	5	4	6	4	5	4	4	5	4	76-290
Tom Watson	Round 1	3	4	4	4	5	4	4	4	4	3	4	3	3	3	4	4	4	3	67
	Round 2	6	3	3	4	5	4	4	4	6	5	3	3	4	4	5	4	6	3	76
	Round 3	4	3	4	4	5	4	4	3	4	3	5	3	4	5	4	3	4	4	70
	Round 4	4	4	4	4	5	5	4	3	5	5	4	4	5	4	4	5	5	3	77-290
Severiano Ballesteros	Round 1	4	4	3	5	6	4	4	4	4	4	3	4	5	5	3	4	5	4	75
	Round 2	4	4	3	4	5	3	4	5	4	4	3	3	5	4	4	3	4	3	69
	Round 3	4	5	4	5	5	4	4	4	4	4	3	5	4	4	4	5	4	4	76
	Round 4	4	3	3	5	5	4	4	3	4	4	3	4	3	5	5	5	4	3	71-291
Warren Bennett	Round 1	5	5	3	4	5	4	4	3	4	4	3	4	4	5	4	4	4	3	72
	Round 2	4	4	4	5	6	4	4	3	3	5	4	3	4	4	4	5	5	3	74
	Round 3	4	4	4	4	5	4	4	3	4	5	4	4	4	3	4	5	5	3	73
	Round 4	4	4	4	4	5	4	5	3	4	5	3	3	4	4	4	4	4	4	72-291
Phil Mickelson	Round 1	5	5	3	4	5	3	4	3	4	3	2	4	4	4	4	4	5	4	70
	Round 2	4	4	4	4	5	4	4	3	5	3	3	3	4	4	5	5	4	3	71
	Round 3	5	5	4	4	4	4	4	3	3	6	4	3	5	5	4	4	7	3	77
	Round 4	5	4	4	4	5	4	4	4	4	4	3	4	4	5	4	4	4	3	73-291
Mark McNulty	Round 1	4	3	4	4	6	4	3	2	3	3	3	4	4	4	4	4	4	4	67
	Round 2	4	4	4	5	7	4	5	3	4	3	4	3	4	5	3	4	6	4	76
	Round 3	2	4	5	6	5	4	4	3	4	4	3	4	4	4	4	5	5	4	74
	Round 4	4	4	4	4	4	4	4	3	4	4	4	4	5	6	4	4	4	4	74-291
Nick Faldo	Round 1	4	4	4	4	4	5	4	4	4	4	3	4	4	6	4	4	5	3	74
	Round 2	3	4	4	3	5	4	3	3	4	3	3	3	4	4	4	5	4	4	67
	Round 3	4	4	4	5	5	4	4	3	4	4	2	6	3	4	5	5	5	4	75
	Round 4	5	4	3	4	4	4	5	3	4	4	3	5	4	6	4	4	5	4	75-291

HOLE		1	2	3	4	5	6	7	8	9	10	11	12	13	14	15	16	17	18	
PAR		4	4	4	4	5	4	4	3	4	4	3	4	4	5	4	4	4	4	TOTAL
Brian Watts	Round 1	3	4	3	4	5	4	4	3	5	4	2	4	5	5	4	5	4	4	72
	Round 2	3	3	4	4	5	4	4	4	4	3	3	4	4	4	4	5	5	4	71
	Round 3	5	5	4	5	6	3	4	3	3	4	3	3	4	5	4	4	4	4	73
	Round 4	4	4	4	4	4	5	3	3	6	5	3	3	3	5	5	5	5	4	75-291
*Gordon Sherry	Round 1	3	4	4	4	4	4	4	3	4	4	3	4	4	5	4	5	4	3	70
	Round 2	4	4	3	5	5	4	4	3	3	4	4	5	4	5	3	4	4	3	71
	Round 3	4	6	4	4	5	4	4	3	3	4	4	3	4	4	4	4	6	4	74
	Round 4	4	4	3	4	5	4	5	3	4	4	4	4	5	6	4	4	5	4	76-291
John Cook	Round 1	4	4	4	4	4	5	3	3	3	4	2	3	5	5	3	4	5	4	69
	Round 2	3	3	4	4	5	4	4	4	3	5	3	3	4	5	4	4	4	4	70
	Round 3	4	4	5	4	6	4	4	3	4	4	3	4	5	5	4	4	4	4	75
	Round 4	4	4	4	4	5	4	4	3	3	4	4	4	5	5	5	5	6	4	77-291
Nick Price	Round 1	4	4	4	5	4	5	3	2	4	4	4	3	4	4	4	5	3	4	70
	Round 2	5	4	4	4	5	6	4	3	3	4	4	4	4	4	4	4	4	4	74
	Round 3	4	4	4	4	5	5	4	3	3	4	3	4	4	4	3	3	5	4	70
	Round 4	4	6	4	4	4	4	4	3	4	5	4	3	5	6	4	5	5	3	77-291
Ian Woosnam	Round 1	4	4	4	4	4	4	3	3	4	4	4	4	4	5	4	4	4	4	71
	Round 2	4	4	4	4	5	4	3	3	3	4	3	4	4	5	5	5	6	4	74
	Round 3	4	4	4	4	5	4	4	4	5	5	3	3	5	5	3	5	5	4	76
	Round 4	4	4	3	4	6	3	4	3	4	4	3	3	4	5	4	4	5	4	71-292
Anders Forsbrand	Round 1	4	4	3	4	5	4	4	3	4	4	3	3	4	5	4	4	5	3	70
	Round 2	4	5	4	5	4	5	4	3	4	4	4	4	5	5	3	4	4	3	74
	Round 3	4	5	4	5	4	4	4	3	5	5	3	4	4	3	4	5	5	4	75
	Round 4	4	4	3	5	4	4	4	3	4	4	3	4	4	5	5	4	5	4	73-292
Mark O'Meara	Round 1	3	4	4	4	5	4	4	2	4	4	3	4	5	5	4	4	5	4	72
	Round 2	4	5	4	4	4	4	4	4	4	4	3	4	4	5	4	4	4	3	72
	Round 3	4	6	3	4	5	4	3	4	3	4	4	3	5	4	5	5	5	4	75
	Round 4	4	4	4	4	4	4	4	4	4	3	4	5	4	5	4	4	5	3	73-292
Tsuneyuki Nakajima	Round 1	4	3	4	5	5	3	4	3	5	4	4	4	4	5	4	4	5	3	73
	Round 2	4	4	4	4	4	4	4	4	4	4	4	4	5	4	3	4	4	4	72
	Round 3	4	4	4	4	5	4	4	4	4	4	3	4	5	4	4	4	4	3	72
	Round 4	5	4	5	4	5	4	4	3	4	4	4	3	5	5	4	4	4	4	75-292
Brian Claar	Round 1	3	4	4	4	4	5	4	4	3	4	3	4	4	5	4	3	5	4	71
	Round 2	4	4	4	4	5	4	5	3	5	4	4	4	5	5	3	4	4	4	75
	Round 3	4	4	4	4	5	4	3	3	3	4	4	4	4	5	4	4	4	4	71
	Round 4	4	4	4	5	6	5	4	4	3	4	3	4	3	4	4	5	5	4	75-292
Ken Green	Round 1	4	4	4	4	5	5	4	2	3	4	2	5	4	5	4	4	4	4	71
	Round 2	5	3	4	5	4	4	4	4	4	3	4	2	5	5	4	4	5	3	72
	Round 3	4	4	4	4	6	5	4	3	5	4	3	4	4	3	3	5	5	3	73
	Round 4	4	5	5	5	4	4	4	3	4	4	3	4	5	5	3	4	6	4	76-292
Jim Gallagher Jnr	Round 1	4	4	4	4	4	4	3	3	3	4	4	5	5	4	3	5	4	2	69
	Round 2	4	4	4	5	6	4	4	4	3	4	3	4	4	5	4	4	6	4	76
	Round 3	4	4	4	5	6	5	4	4	5	3	3	4	4	4	4	4	4	4	75
	Round 4	4	4	4	4	4	4	4	3	4	5	3	5	3	5	4	4	5	4	73-293
Peter O'Malley	Round 1	4	5	3	4	7	4	4	3	4	4	3	4	3	4	4	4	4	3	71
	Round 2	4	4	3	4	5	3	5	4	4	6	4	4	3	4	4	4	5	3	73
	Round 3	4	5	4	5	6	4	4	4	4	4	3	3	3	5	4	4	5	3	74
	Round 4	3	4	4	4	4	4	4	3	4	4	4	4	5	5	5	5	5	4	75-293

HOLE		1	2	3	4	5	6	7	8	9	10	11	12	13	14	15	16	17	18	
PAR		4	4	4	4	5	4	4	3	4	4	3	4	4	5	4	4	4	4	TOTAL
Russell Claydon	Round 1	4	3	3	4	5	4	3	3	4	4	3	5	4	5	4	4	5	3	70
	Round 2	3	4	3	5	5	5	5	3	4	4	4	4	4	5	3	5	5	3	74
	Round 3	4	4	4	4	5	4	4	4	4	4	3	4	4	3	4	4	4	4	71
	Round 4	4	5	4	4	6	4	5	4	4	5	3	4	4	5	4	4	5	4	78-293
Peter Senior	Round 1	4	4	3	4	5	4	4	3	4	4	3	3	5	5	4	3	5	4	71
	Round 2	4	4	4	5	6	4	4	4	3	4	4	4	4	4	4	4	5	4	75
	Round 3	4	5	6	4	5	4	4	3	4	4	4	5	5	5	5	5	3	3	78
	Round 4	3	4	3	4	4	4	4	3	4	4	3	5	4	5	3	5	4	4	70-294
Paul Broadhurst	Round 1	4	4	4	4	5	5	4	4	4	3	3	4	4	5	4	4	5	3	73
	Round 2	4	4	3	5	5	4	4	3	4	4	3	3	6	4	4	4	5	3	72
	Round 3	5	4	4	5	7	4	4	4	4	4	2	3	4	6	5	3	4	4	76
	Round 4	3	4	4	4	5	4	4	3	4	4	2	5	5	6	4	4	5	3	73-294
Derrick Cooper	Round 1	4	5	4	4	5	4	4	3	4	3	3	4	5	4	3	4	4	4	71
	Round 2	6	5	3	4	5	4	4	4	5	4	3	3	4	4	6	4	4	4	76
	Round 3	5	5	4	5	5	4	4	3	3	4	3	4	4	4	4	5	4	4	74
	Round 4	4	3	4	4	5	4	4	3	4	4	3	4	4	5	5	4	5	4	73-294
Eduardo Herrera	Round 1	4	5	4	4	5	3	4	3	4	6	3	4	4	5	4	4	5	3	74
	Round 2	4	4	4	4	5	5	4	3	4	4	3	3	4	4	4	6	4	3	72
	Round 3	3	4	4	4	6	4	4	3	4	5	3	4	4	4	4	5	4	4	73
	Round 4	4	5	4	4	5	4	4	4	4	4	4	5	3	5	4	3	5	4	75-294
Tom Kite	Round 1	5	4	4	4	5	4	4	3	4	3	4	4	4	5	4	4	4	3	72
	Round 2	4	4	4	5	5	4	5	4	5	4	4	3	3	6	4	3	5	4	76
	Round 3	4	5	4	5	5	3	5	3	4	4	3	3	3	5	3	4	4	4	71
	Round 4	3	5	4	4	4	4	4	4	4	4	4	5	5	4	4	5	4	5	75-294
Paul Lawrie	Round 1	4	4	3	4	4	4	4	3	4	4	4	4	5	4	4	5	5	4	73
	Round 2	4	3	4	5	5	4	4	5	5	4	3	4	3	3	4	4	4	3	71
	Round 3	5	4	4	5	5	4	4	3	4	3	3	5	5	4	4	4	4	4	74
	Round 4	4	5	3	4	4	4	4	3	5	6	3	4	3	5	5	4	5	5	76-294
Martin Gates	Round 1	5	4	3	4	5	4	4	3	4	4	3	4	4	5	4	4	5	4	73
	Round 2	5	4	4	4	5	4	3	3	3	4	4	3	5	4	4	5	6	3	73
	Round 3	4	3	4	4	5	3	4	3	3	6	3	3	5	4	5	4	5	4	72
	Round 4	4	5	4	4	5	4	4	4	4	3	3	4	4	6	5	5	4	4	76-294
Raymond Floyd	Round 1	4	4	4	4	4	5	3	2	4	4	4	4	5	4	4	5	4	4	72
	Round 2	6	4	4	4	4	4	4	4	4	5	3	3	3	4	4	4	5	5	74
	Round 3	4	5	3	4	6	3	4	4	4	4	3	4	4	5	4	4	4	3	72
	Round 4	5	4	3	4	4	4	5	4	4	3	4	5	4	5	5	5	4	4	76-294
Justin Leonard	Round 1	5	4	4	4	4	5	4	4	4	4	3	4	3	5	4	5	4	3	73
	Round 2	3	4	4	4	4	4	4	3	4	4	3	3	4	3	4	4	4	4	67
	Round 3	4	4	4	5	7	5	4	3	4	4	3	3	5	4	4	4	6	4	77
	Round 4	4	4	4	4	5	5	4	3	4	4	4	5	5	4	5	5	4	4	77-294
David Gilford	Round 1	4	4	4	4	5	4	3	3	4	4	2	4	3	5	4	4	4	4	69
	Round 2	4	4	4	4	5	4	4	3	3	4	3	4	5	5	4	4	5	3	72
	Round 3	4	6	4	4	5	5	4	3	4	4	4	4	4	3	5	5	3	4	75
	Round 4	5	5	4	5	4	5	4	3	4	4	4	6	4	5	4	4	5	3	78-294
Peter Baker	Round 1	4	3	3	4	4	4	4	3	4	4	3	4	4	4	4	5	5	4	70
	Round 2	3	5	4	4	5	4	5	3	3	4	4	3	5	5	5	4	5	3	74
	Round 3	5	4	5	5	7	5	4	3	3	4	3	4	5	4	6	5	5	4	81
	Round 4	4	4	4	4	5	4	4	3	4	3	4	4	4	4	4	4	4	3	70-295

HOLE		1	2	3	4	5	6	7	8	9	10	11	12	13	14	15	16	17	18	
PAR		4	4	4	4	5	4	4	3	4	4	3	4	4	5	4	4	4	4	TOTAL
Jeff Maggert	Round 1	4	4	4	5	6	3	4	2	4	4	3	4	3	5	5	5	6	4	75
	Round 2	4	4	3	5	5	4	4	3	3	4	4	3	4	4	4	4	5	3	70
	Round 3	5	4	5	4	6	4	5	3	4	4	4	4	4	6	4	4	5	3	78
	Round 4	3	4	4	4	4	4	4	4	4	4	4	5	4	6	4	3	3	4	72-295
Jonathan Lomas	Round 1	3	4	4	4	4	5	4	3	4	4	4	5	5	5	4	4	4	4	74
	Round 2	4	3	3	5	5	5	4	4	4	4	3	4	5	5	4	4	4	3	73
	Round 3	4	5	4	5	5	4	4	3	4	4	5	3	5	4	3	4	6	3	75
	Round 4	4	4	4	4	4	3	4	3	4	4	3	4	5	6	5	4	4	4	73-295
Frank Nobilo	Round 1	3	4	3	4	4	3	4	2	5	3	3	4	5	5	4	4	6	4	70
	Round 2	4	4	4	4	5	4	4	3	4	4	6	4	3	4	4	3	4	3	71
	Round 3	5	5	4	5	5	5	5	4	4	4	2	5	5	5	4	5	4	4	80
	Round 4	4	4	4	4	5	4	4	3	4	4	3	4	5	5	4	4	5	4	74-295
Gary Player	Round 1	3	3	5	4	5	4	4	4	3	4	3	4	4	5	4	5	4	3	71
	Round 2	4	5	4	4	5	4	3	3	4	4	3	4	4	5	4	4	5	4	73
	Round 3	6	4	4	5	5	5	4	4	4	4	2	4	4	6	4	4	4	4	77
	Round 4	4	5	4	4	5	4	4	3	4	4	4	3	4	5	4	5	4	4	74-295
Olle Karlsson	Round 1	3	4	3	4	5	3	4	3	4	4	5	4	5	4	4	3	5	4	71
	Round 2	4	4	4	4	5	4	4	3	4	4	4	6	5	4	4	3	4	6	76
	Round 3	4	4	4	4	5	4	4	2	6	5	4	3	4	5	3	4	4	4	73
	Round 4	3	4	4	4	5	5	4	4	4	4	3	4	4	6	4	5	4	4	75-295
Mats Hallberg	Round 1	4	4	3	4	5	5	4	3	4	4	3	3	4	3	4	4	4	3	68
	Round 2	4	4	4	4	5	4	5	4	4	4	3	4	5	4	4	5	6	3	76
	Round 3	4	4	5	4	5	4	4	4	6	4	3	3	4	5	4	5	4	3	75
	Round 4	4	5	3	4	5	4	4	5	4	4	4	5	4	5	4	4	5	3	76-295
Scott Hoch	Round 1	5	4	4	4	5	5	4	3	3	4	3	4	5	5	4	4	4	4	74
	Round 2	4	4	3	4	5	4	4	3	4	4	6	4	4	4	4	4	4	3	72
	Round 3	4	5	3	5	5	4	3	4	3	5	3	3	5	4	4	5	5	3	73
	Round 4	4	4	4	5	4	5	5	5	4	4	4	5	3	4	4	4	5	3	76-295
Gary Hallberg	Round 1	3	4	4	4	4	4	4	3	4	4	3	4	5	5	4	4	5	4	72
	Round 2	5	4	3	4	5	4	4	2	3	4	4	4	4	7	4	5	4	4	74
	Round 3	4	5	4	4	5	4	4	3	4	4	3	4	5	4	4	4	4	3	72
	Round 4	4	4	4	4	6	3	5	3	4	5	4	4	4	6	5	4	5	3	77-295
Jose Rivero	Round 1	4	4	4	4	5	4	4	2	4	4	3	3	4	5	4	4	4	4	70
	Round 2	4	4	4	4	4	4	4	3	4	4	4	4	5	3	5	4	4	4	72
	Round 3	4	4	5	4	5	5	4	3	4	5	3	4	4	4	4	5	5	3	75
	Round 4	4	4	5	3	5	3	4	4	4	5	6	4	4	5	4	5	5	4	78-295
*Tiger Woods	Round 1	4	7	4	4	5	4	4	3	4	3	3	4	4	4	4	4	5	4	74
	Round 2	4	4	3	5	7	4	4	3	3	4	3	3	4	5	4	3	4	4	71
	Round 3	4	4	3	5	5	4	3	3	3	4	4	3	5	6	4	4	5	3	72
	Round 4	4	6	4	4	6	5	4	4	4	4	3	4	5	5	4	4	4	4	78-295
Ryoken Kawagishi	Round 1	4	3	4	4	4	4	5	3	4	3	4	4	5	4	4	4	5	4	72
	Round 2	4	4	3	4	6	4	4	3	4	4	5	4	5	4	4	4	6	4	76
	Round 3	5	4	5	6	6	4	4	3	5	4	4	4	5	4	4	5	4	4	80
	Round 4	4	4	3	4	5	3	4	4	4	4	3	4	3	4	4	3	5	3	68-296
Patrick Burke	Round 1	4	5	4	5	5	4	4	3	3	4	3	5	4	6	4	4	4	4	75
	Round 2	4	4	4	4	6	4	5	3	3	3	4	4	4	4	4	4	4	4	72
	Round 3	4	4	3	5	5	5	6	3	4	4	3	4	6	5	4	4	5	4	78
	Round 4	4	4	5	3	6	4	5	2	3	4	3	4	4	4	4	4	4	4	71-296

HOLE		1	2	3	4	5	6	7	8	9	10	11	12	13	14	15	16	17	18	
PAR		4	4	4	4	5	4	4	3	4	4	3	4	4	5	4	4	4	4	TOTAL
Jack Nicklaus	Round 1	5	5	4	4	4	4	4	3	4	4	3	5	5	10	3	4	4	3	78
	Round 2	4	4	3	3	5	4	4	3	4	4	3	4	4	5	4	4	4	4	70
	Round 3	5	3	4	5	7	4	4	3	5	4	3	4	4	5	4	4	5	4	77
	Round 4	4	4	4	5	4	4	4	3	4	4	3	4	4	5	4	3	5	3	71-296
Bob Lohr	Round 1	5	4	4	4	5	4	4	3	4	4	4	5	4	5	4	4	5	4	76
	Round 2	4	3	4	4	4	4	4	3	4	4	3	4	5	3	4	4	4	3	68
	Round 3	5	5	4	5	5	5	5	3	5	4	3	5	4	5	4	4	5	3	79
	Round 4	4	3	4	4	4	4	5	4	4	4	3	4	4	5	4	5	4	4	73-296
Jarmo Sandelin	Round 1	4	4	4	4	4	4	5	4	4	4	4	3	4	5	4	5	6	3	75
	Round 2	4	4	4	4	4	4	4	3	4	4	4	4	4	4	3	4	6	3	71
	Round 3	4	4	5	5	5	4	3	3	4	4	5	4	6	5	4	4	4	4	77
	Round 4	4	4	4	4	4	4	4	3	4	4	4	3	5	5	4	4	5	4	73-296
Sandy Lyle	Round 1	4	4	3	4	5	3	4	3	4	4	3	4	4	5	4	4	5	4	71
	Round 2	4	5	4	4	5	3	4	3	3	4	4	3	4	5	3	4	5	4	71
	Round 3	5	5	3	4	5	5	4	4	5	6	3	3	7	4	4	4	5	3	79
	Round 4	4	4	3	4	4	5	5	4	4	4	5	3	4	5	4	4	5	4	75-296
Steve Lowery	Round 1	4	4	4	4	4	4	3	3	3	4	3	3	5	5	4	5	3	4	69
	Round 2	4	3	4	5	5	4	5	3	4	4	3	3	5	4	4	6	4	4	74
	Round 3	5	6	4	4	5	4	5	3	4	4	3	4	5	5	5	4	3	3	76
	Round 4	4	3	4	4	5	4	5	4	4	4	3	4	4	6	4	4	7	4	77-296
Dean Robertson	Round 1	4	4	4	4	4	4	4	3	4	4	3	4	4	4	4	4	5	4	71
	Round 2	4	5	4	5	5	4	4	3	4	3	4	4	4	4	4	4	4	4	73
	Round 3	4	4	5	4	5	3	5	3	3	5	3	4	5	5	4	4	5	3	74
	Round 4	5	4	5	4	4	5	4	3	4	4	3	4	4	5	6	5	6	3	78-296
Jay Haas	Round 1	5	5	4	4	6	5	4	3	4	4	3	3	4	5	4	4	5	4	76
	Round 2	4	4	3	4	4	4	4	3	3	4	3	4	4	5	4	6	5	4	72
	Round 3	4	4	4	5	5	4	4	3	3	4	3	4	4	3	4	4	4	4	70
	Round 4	4	5	4	5	5	5	5	4	4	3	5	4	4	5	4	4	4	4	78-296
Miguel Angel Jimenez	Round 1	4	4	4	5	6	4	5	3	3	4	3	5	5	4	3	4	5	4	75
	Round 2	4	4	4	4	5	4	4	3	4	4	6	4	4	4	4	4	4	3	73
	Round 3	4	4	3	4	6	5	4	3	4	3	4	5	5	4	4	4	6	4	76
	Round 4	3	4	4	4	5	4	4	3	4	4	4	5	3	6	4	4	4	4	73-297
Mark Davis	Round 1	4	2	4	3	5	4	4	4	4	4	3	4	5	4	4	4	5	5	74
	Round 2	4	4	3	4	5	4	4	3	4	4	4	3	4	4	4	5	4	4	71
	Round 3	5	4	4	5	5	5	5	3	3	5	3	5	5	4	4	3	5	3	76
	Round 4	4	4	4	4	4	5	4	3	4	4	3	5	5	5	5	5	4	4	76-297
Jay Delsing	Round 1	4	4	4	4	4	5	4	3	4	5	3	4	4	4	5	4	4	3	72
	Round 2	4	4	5	5	4	4	5	3	3	4	4	4	3	5	4	4	6	4	75
	Round 3	3	5	5	4	6	4	4	2	3	4	4	4	3	5	4	4	5	4	73
	Round 4	4	4	4	4	5	5	3	4	4	4	4	5	5	5	4	4	5	4	77-297
Eduardo Romero	Round 1	3	5	5	4	5	4	4	4	4	4	4	3	4	4	5	4	4	4	74
	Round 2	4	4	4	4	5	4	4	4	3	4	5	4	4	5	3	4	5	4	74
	Round 3	5	4	4	5	4	4	4	3	4	4	3	3	4	4	4	5	5	3	72
	Round 4	5	4	4	4	5	4	4	3	4	4	4	5	5	5	4	4	5	4	77-297
Gene Sauers	Round 1	3	4	4	4	5	4	4	3	4	4	3	4	4	4	4	4	4	3	69
	Round 2	4	4	5	4	4	5	5	3	3	4	4	4	4	5	4	4	4	3	73
	Round 3	4	4	4	5	6	4	4	3	4	4	3	4	5	4	4	4	5	4	75
	Round 4	3	5	5	5	4	3	5	3	5	5	3	5	4	5	5	6	5	4	80-297

HOLE		1	2	3	4	5	6	7	8	9	10	11	12	13	14	15	16	17	18	
PAR		4	4	4	4	5	4	4	3	4	4	3	4	4	5	4	4	4	4	TOTAL
Wayne Riley	Round 1	4	4	4	4	4	4	4	3	4	4	2	5	5	4	4	4	4	3	70
	Round 2	5	5	4	4	4	4	3	4	3	3	4	3	4	4	5	4	6	3	72
	Round 3	5	4	3	3	7	4	4	3	5	5	4	3	4	4	4	4	5	4	75
	Round 4	5	4	4	5	4	4	5	4	3	5	4	5	4	5	4	5	7	3	80-297
John Hawksworth	Round 1	3	4	4	5	4	5	4	3	4	4	3	4	4	5	4	4	5	4	73
	Round 2	4	4	4	4	5	5	4	3	4	4	3	4	4	5	4	5	5	3	74
	Round 3	4	4	4	6	5	5	4	2	4	3	3	4	5	4	4	5	5	4	75
	Round 4	4	4	5	4	4	4	4	3	4	4	4	4	5	5	5	4	5	4	76-298
Bill Longmuir	Round 1	4	3	4	4	5	5	5	3	3	4	3	4	4	5	4	4	5	3	72
	Round 2	5	4	3	5	5	5	3	3	4	4	4	4	4	4	5	6	4	4	76
	Round 3	3	4	4	4	6	4	4	2	5	5	3	2	5	5	4	4	5	3	72
	Round 4	5	4	4	4	4	5	5	3	4	5	4	4	5	4	4	4	6	4	78-298
Lee Westwood	Round 1	4	4	3	4	5	4	4	3	4	4	3	4	4	4	5	4	4	4	71
	Round 2	4	4	4	4	4	5	6	3	4	3	3	4	3	4	4	5	4	4	72
	Round 3	5	6	4	5	5	4	5	3	5	4	4	3	4	5	4	5	7	4	82
	Round 4	3	4	4	4	6	4	5	3	3	6	3	4	4	4	4	4	5	4	74-299
Jose Coceres	Round 1	3	4	4	4	4	4	5	3	4	5	3	3	4	5	3	4	5	4	71
	Round 2	4	5	4	4	5	4	5	3	4	4	4	2	5	5	4	5	5	4	76
	Round 3	5	4	4	6	5	4	4	4	5	4	4	3	5	4	4	4	5	4	78
	Round 4	4	4	4	4	4	4	4	3	3	4	3	4	5	4	5	4	7	4	74-299
Simon Burnell	Round 1	4	5	3	4	6	5	4	3	3	4	2	4	4	4	4	4	5	4	72
	Round 2	3	4	5	4	5	4	3	3	5	4	4	4	5	5	4	4	6	4	76
	Round 3	4	4	4	4	5	4	4	3	4	4	3	4	4	6	5	4	5	4	75
	Round 4	4	4	4	4	5	4	5	3	4	4	3	4	4	6	5	5	4	5	77-300
Davis Love III	Round 1	4	4	4	3	4	4	4	3	4	3	4	4	5	5	3	4	5	3	70
	Round 2	4	5	4	5	4	5	4	3	5	4	3	4	4	5	4	5	5	5	78
	Round 3	4	4	4	4	5	4	4	4	4	5	3	4	5	4	4	3	5	4	74
	Round 4	4	4	4	4	5	4	5	4	5	4	3	4	4	5	5	5	6	3	78-300
*Gary Clark	Round 1	4	4	3	5	3	4	5	3	3	4	3	4	4	5	4	5	4	4	71
	Round 2	4	4	4	4	6	4	3	3	3	7	5	4	5	4	4	4	4	4	76
	Round 3	5	4	4	5	5	4	4	2	5	4	8	4	4	5	4	4	5	4	80
	Round 4	4	4	4	3	4	5	4	3	5	4	3	4	5	6	4	4	4	4	74-301
Don Pooley	Round 1	5	4	4	5	5	5	5	3	4	4	3	4	5	4	4	4	4	4	76
	Round 2	4	5	4	5	4	4	4	3	4	3	4	4	3	5	4	4	4	3	71
	Round 3	5	4	5	6	5	6	4	3	4	4	4	5	4	4	4	4	5	4	80
	Round 4	4	4	4	4	5	4	4	3	4	5	3	5	5	5	4	5	4	3	75-302
Mark Nichols	Round 1	5	4	4	4	5	5	4	2	4	4	4	4	5	5	4	4	5	3	75
	Round 2	4	4	3	4	5	3	4	3	3	3	3	4	4	5	4	4	5	3	68
	Round 3	4	5	4	5	6	6	4	4	2	4	3	4	4	5	4	5	5	4	78
	Round 4	4	4	4	4	8	4	4	4	4	4	4	5	4	6	4	6	5	3	81-302
Pedro Linhart	Round 1	4	5	3	4	4	4	4	2	4	3	4	4	4	6	4	5	4	4	72
	Round 2	4	3	5	4	6	4	4	3	4	4	3	4	6	5	4	3	5	4	75
	Round 3	3	4	5	4	6	4	5	4	5	4	3	4	4	5	4	4	5	4	77
	Round 4	4	5	4	4	5	4	5	4	4	4	5	4	4	7	4	5	4	3	79-303

HOLE		1	2	3	4	5	6	7	8	9	10	11	12	13	14	15	16	17	18	
PAR		4	4	4	4	5	4	4	3	4	4	3	4	4	5	4	4	4	4	TOTAL

NON QUALIFIERS AFTER 36 HOLES

Player	Round	1	2	3	4	5	6	7	8	9	10	11	12	13	14	15	16	17	18	Total
John Watson	Round 1	4	5	5	4	7	4	5	3	4	4	3	4	4	5	4	3	5	3	76
	Round 2	4	5	4	4	5	4	5	3	4	4	3	4	4	4	4	4	4	4	73-149
Bob Tway	Round 1	4	4	4	4	6	3	3	3	4	5	2	4	5	4	4	3	5	4	71
	Round 2	4	6	4	5	5	3	4	4	4	4	4	4	5	5	4	4	5	4	78-149
Paul Azinger	Round 1	4	5	4	4	4	5	4	3	4	4	3	4	4	5	4	5	4	4	74
	Round 2	4	6	4	4	5	4	4	3	5	4	3	5	3	4	5	4	3	5	75-149
Mike Springer	Round 1	5	4	4	5	4	4	4	3	3	4	4	5	5	5	4	4	4	4	75
	Round 2	4	5	4	5	5	4	3	4	4	4	4	3	5	5	4	3	5	3	74-149
Masashi Ozaki	Round 1	4	5	4	3	4	4	4	2	4	4	3	4	5	5	4	3	5	3	70
	Round 2	6	4	4	4	5	5	5	3	3	4	4	4	4	5	4	5	5	5	79-149
Bob Charles	Round 1	4	3	5	4	5	4	4	3	4	4	4	4	4	4	4	4	5	4	73
	Round 2	4	4	4	5	5	4	5	4	4	4	4	5	4	5	4	4	4	3	76-149
Scott Simpson	Round 1	4	4	3	4	5	4	4	3	4	4	5	4	5	4	4	4	4	3	72
	Round 2	5	5	4	4	6	5	4	3	5	5	4	3	4	4	4	4	4	4	77-149
Howard Clark	Round 1	5	4	4	4	4	5	5	3	4	4	3	4	5	5	5	4	4	4	76
	Round 2	4	4	4	4	4	4	5	4	4	4	3	5	4	5	4	4	3	4	73-149
John Morse	Round 1	4	4	4	4	5	5	4	4	4	4	3	4	4	5	4	4	6	3	75
	Round 2	4	4	4	4	5	5	4	3	4	4	3	4	7	4	4	4	4	3	74-149
Curtis Strange	Round 1	4	5	3	4	4	4	4	3	4	4	3	4	5	5	4	5	4	4	73
	Round 2	4	4	4	5	4	6	4	3	4	5	3	3	5	5	4	5	5	3	76-149
Peter Fowler	Round 1	4	4	4	5	4	5	5	4	4	4	3	3	4	5	4	4	4	4	74
	Round 2	4	4	5	5	5	3	5	4	4	4	3	5	4	5	4	4	4	3	75-149
Nigel Graves	Round 1	3	5	4	3	6	5	4	3	5	5	2	4	4	4	4	4	4	3	72
	Round 2	4	3	4	5	7	5	4	3	4	4	3	3	7	5	4	4	4	4	77-149
Jamie Spence	Round 1	4	6	4	4	5	5	4	4	4	4	3	4	5	6	4	4	4	3	77
	Round 2	3	4	5	4	5	4	4	3	4	4	3	4	4	6	4	5	4	3	73-150
Mark Roe	Round 1	4	4	4	4	5	3	4	3	4	4	3	4	4	6	5	4	6	4	75
	Round 2	4	5	4	4	4	4	4	4	3	4	4	4	4	5	3	5	5	5	75-150
Stephen Leaney	Round 1	4	4	4	4	5	4	5	3	4	4	4	3	4	8	4	4	4	4	76
	Round 2	6	4	5	4	5	5	4	4	4	4	3	3	3	4	4	4	4	4	74-150
Loren Roberts	Round 1	4	4	4	4	4	5	4	3	4	5	3	4	5	5	4	4	5	5	76
	Round 2	4	4	4	6	5	5	4	4	4	3	4	3	4	4	3	4	5	4	74-150
Wayne Grady	Round 1	4	5	4	5	5	4	5	3	3	4	3	4	5	4	3	4	6	4	75
	Round 2	3	4	4	5	5	4	5	3	3	4	3	4	5	5	4	5	5	4	75-150
Tony Johnstone	Round 1	3	4	4	5	6	4	4	3	4	4	4	4	5	5	4	4	4	4	75
	Round 2	4	4	4	4	5	4	4	3	4	4	4	5	4	5	4	4	5	4	75-150
Brandt Jobe	Round 1	3	5	3	4	4	5	5	3	4	4	3	3	5	4	5	5	5	4	74
	Round 2	4	5	4	4	5	4	5	3	4	4	3	4	6	5	4	4	4	4	76-150
Colin Montgomerie	Round 1	4	5	4	4	4	5	3	4	4	4	4	4	4	4	4	5	5	4	75
	Round 2	4	4	4	4	6	4	4	4	4	5	4	3	3	5	4	4	5	4	75-150
Craig Stadler	Round 1	4	6	3	3	4	4	4	4	4	4	3	4	5	5	4	4	5	4	74
	Round 2	5	4	4	4	6	4	4	4	4	4	5	4	4	4	3	4	5	4	76-150
Mark McCumber	Round 1	4	4	4	4	5	4	3	3	4	4	3	4	5	4	4	4	5	5	73
	Round 2	5	6	3	6	5	4	4	4	4	4	4	4	4	4	4	4	5	3	77-150
Miguel Martin	Round 1	4	4	4	5	6	4	4	3	3	5	3	5	4	5	3	4	4	3	73
	Round 2	4	5	4	5	5	5	3	3	4	4	3	4	4	6	4	4	6	4	77-150

HOLE		1	2	3	4	5	6	7	8	9	10	11	12	13	14	15	16	17	18	TOTAL
PAR		4	4	4	4	5	4	4	3	4	4	3	4	5	4	4	4	4	4	TOTAL
Michel Besanceney	Round 1	4	4	4	4	5	4	3	3	4	4	3	4	5	5	3	5	5	4	73
	Round 2	5	5	4	4	4	5	4	4	5	3	4	4	4	6	4	4	5	3	77-150
Larry Mize	Round 1	4	4	3	3	5	4	4	3	5	4	3	4	6	5	5	4	4	4	74
	Round 2	4	4	5	4	5	4	5	4	4	4	4	4	5	5	4	4	4	4	77-151
Tom Weiskopf	Round 1	4	6	4	5	4	5	5	2	4	4	3	4	4	5	4	3	6	4	76
	Round 2	4	4	3	4	5	5	4	3	6	4	4	4	4	5	5	4	4	3	75-151
Michael Clayton	Round 1	3	4	4	4	5	4	4	4	4	4	3	5	4	5	4	4	5	4	74
	Round 2	3	6	5	4	5	5	4	3	3	4	4	4	4	5	4	4	4	5	77-151
Andrew Crerar	Round 1	5	5	4	4	5	5	3	3	4	4	3	5	5	6	3	4	4	5	77
	Round 2	4	4	4	4	4	5	4	3	4	4	4	3	4	5	4	4	5	5	74-151
*Stephen Gallacher	Round 1	4	3	4	4	5	5	5	3	4	4	3	4	5	4	4	4	4	3	72
	Round 2	4	4	4	5	5	4	5	2	4	5	4	6	4	5	4	4	7	3	79-151
Tom Wargo	Round 1	4	4	3	4	5	4	4	3	3	4	4	4	5	4	4	4	5	4	72
	Round 2	4	5	3	4	5	4	4	4	6	4	3	5	4	6	4	5	4	5	79-151
Robert Karlsson	Round 1	4	4	4	5	6	4	4	4	4	4	3	4	6	4	3	5	5	4	77
	Round 2	4	4	5	4	5	3	5	4	5	4	4	3	4	4	4	3	5	4	74-151
Paul Carman	Round 1	4	3	4	4	4	4	4	4	4	5	3	4	4	4	4	4	5	4	72
	Round 2	4	5	4	5	6	5	6	4	5	4	3	4	4	5	3	4	4	4	79-151
John Bickerton	Round 1	4	4	3	4	4	5	3	3	3	4	3	4	5	5	5	4	5	3	71
	Round 2	4	6	4	5	5	4	4	4	4	4	4	5	4	5	4	3	7	4	80-151
Brad Bryant	Round 1	4	5	4	4	7	5	4	3	4	4	3	3	6	4	4	5	4	5	78
	Round 2	5	6	4	4	5	4	4	3	4	4	3	4	4	5	5	4	3	3	74-152
Carl Mason	Round 1	3	4	4	4	4	4	4	4	4	4	3	4	4	5	6	5	4	5	75
	Round 2	4	4	4	5	5	5	4	3	4	4	3	4	5	5	4	4	6	4	77-152
Billy Andrade	Round 1	4	4	4	5	4	4	4	3	4	4	4	4	5	5	4	4	5	5	76
	Round 2	4	5	4	5	5	4	4	3	3	4	4	4	4	4	6	4	5	4	76-152
Lee Trevino	Round 1	4	5	3	4	5	4	4	4	4	4	3	4	5	6	4	4	5	3	75
	Round 2	4	5	4	4	5	4	4	3	3	4	5	5	4	6	4	5	4	4	77-152
Ian Baker-Finch	Round 1	6	5	4	4	5	4	4	3	4	3	3	4	6	4	4	4	6	4	77
	Round 2	4	5	4	4	5	4	4	4	4	4	4	3	4	5	4	5	5	4	76-153
Tohru Suzuki	Round 1	4	4	4	5	6	4	3	3	4	4	4	6	7	6	4	4	4	4	80
	Round 2	4	4	3	5	5	4	5	3	4	4	2	3	6	6	4	4	4	3	73-153
Ronan Rafferty	Round 1	4	4	4	5	5	4	3	2	4	3	3	6	5	5	4	5	5	4	75
	Round 2	4	4	4	5	5	3	4	4	5	5	3	4	5	4	4	5	6	4	78-153
Adam Tillman	Round 1	4	4	4	5	5	4	4	4	4	4	3	4	4	5	4	5	4	4	75
	Round 2	4	5	3	4	4	4	3	4	4	4	5	4	3	7	3	6	6	5	78-153
John Wither	Round 1	4	6	4	4	4	5	4	3	4	4	3	4	4	6	4	4	4	4	75
	Round 2	4	6	4	4	5	5	5	4	4	3	3	3	5	6	4	4	5	3	78-153
Mathias Gronberg	Round 1	4	4	4	5	5	5	5	3	5	4	3	4	5	5	5	6	5	4	81
	Round 2	5	6	4	4	5	4	4	3	4	4	4	4	4	3	4	3	4	3	72-153
Kazuhiro Takami	Round 1	4	4	4	5	4	6	4	4	5	4	3	4	4	5	4	4	4	4	76
	Round 2	4	5	6	5	5	5	5	3	4	4	3	3	5	4	4	3	5	4	77-153
Craig Parry	Round 1	5	5	3	4	5	4	3	3	4	5	3	4	4	5	4	5	5	5	76
	Round 2	3	5	3	4	5	4	6	3	5	3	4	5	5	4	4	4	6	4	77-153
Russell Weir	Round 1	3	4	4	4	6	4	4	3	3	4	4	4	4	4	4	4	4	4	71
	Round 2	5	5	5	5	5	4	4	3	4	4	4	4	4	5	8	4	5	4	82-153
Neil Roderick	Round 1	4	5	5	5	4	4	4	3	4	4	3	4	4	6	4	4	4	3	74
	Round 2	4	4	4	5	5	4	4	4	5	4	5	3	5	4	5	5	4	5	79-153

HOLE		1	2	3	4	5	6	7	8	9	10	11	12	13	14	15	16	17	18	
PAR		4	4	4	4	5	4	4	3	4	4	3	4	4	5	4	4	4	4	TOTAL
Richard Boxall	Round 1	3	5	3	3	4	4	5	3	4	4	4	3	4	5	5	3	6	4	72
	Round 2	4	5	4	5	5	4	5	5	4	4	3	4	4	4	5	8	4	4	81-153
Fredrik Andersson	Round 1	4	4	4	5	5	4	4	3	4	4	3	4	5	6	4	5	5	4	77
	Round 2	5	5	4	5	5	5	4	3	4	4	2	3	5	5	4	4	4	5	76-153
Martyn Thompson	Round 1	4	4	4	4	4	5	6	3	5	4	3	4	4	6	4	4	4	4	76
	Round 2	4	5	4	5	6	5	4	3	4	5	4	4	4	5	4	4	5	4	79-155
Arnold Palmer	Round 1	5	6	4	5	6	4	4	3	5	5	4	4	6	6	4	4	4	4	83
	Round 2	4	4	5	4	6	4	3	3	4	4	4	4	4	4	4	5	5	4	75-158
Brandel Chamblee	Round 1	4	4	4	4	6	5	5	4	5	4	3	4	4	5	5	5	5	4	80
	Round 2	6	4	6	4	5	4	3	4	4	4	4	4	5	5	4	4	5	3	78-158
Paul Mayo	Round 1	3	4	3	5	5	6	4	4	4	4	3	4	5	5	5	5	4	4	77
	Round 2	4	4	4	6	8	7	4	4	3	4	4	5	4	4	4	4	5	4	82-159
Gary Stafford	Round 1	4	5	5	4	5	5	4	3	4	4	3	4	6	5	4	4	4	5	78
	Round 2	5	4	5	5	6	4	4	4	5	4	4	5	5	5	5	4	5	5	84-162
Andrew Oldcorn	Round 1	4	4	4	5	5	4	4	4	3	3	3	4	4	6	4	4	4	4	73
Philip Walton	Round 1	4	4	3	4	5	5	4	3	4	4	3	4	7	5	3	4	4	5	75